Making Learning
Job-Embedded

BRIDGING THEORY AND PRACTICE

This international series reflects the latest cutting-edge theories and practices in school leadership. Uniquely, we include books that bridge the perennial divide between theory and practice. The series motto is framed after Kurt Lewin's famous statement, and we paraphrase, that there is no sound theory without practice, and no good practice that is not framed on some theory.

Making Learning Job-Embedded: Cases from the Field of Instructional Leadership

Edited by
Sally J. Zepeda

ROWMAN & LITTLEFIELD
Lanham • Boulder • New York • London

Published by Rowman & Littlefield
A wholly owned subsidiary of The Rowman & Littlefield Publishing Group, Inc.
4501 Forbes Boulevard, Suite 200, Lanham, Maryland 20706
www.rowman.com

Unit A, Whitacre Mews, 26-34 Stannary Street, London SE11 4AB

Copyright © 2018 by Sally J. Zepeda

All rights reserved. No part of this book may be reproduced in any form or by any electronic or mechanical means, including information storage and retrieval systems, without written permission from the publisher, except by a reviewer who may quote passages in a review.

British Library Cataloguing in Publication Information Available

Library of Congress Cataloging-in-Publication Data Is Available

ISBN: 978-1-4758-3833-6 (cloth: alk. paper)
ISBN: 978-1-4758-3834-3 (paper: alk. paper)
ISBN: 978-1-4758-3835-0 (electronic)

Contents

Series Editor's Introduction — vii

Volume Introduction — xi

Preface — xiii

Acknowledgments — xv

Introduction — 1

Chapter 1: Getting to Job-Embedded Learning — 3
Sally J. Zepeda

Chapter 2: Understanding the Job-Embedded Learning Experiences of Middle School Teachers — 15
Brandi Wade Worsham

Chapter 3: Creating Coherence Between Teacher Evaluation and Ongoing Teacher Learning by Engaging in Collegial Goal Groups — 35
Jen Cole

Chapter 4: The Impact of Incoherent Professional Learning on Standards-Based Reform — 55
Michael P. Cassidy

Chapter 5: Professional Development: Using Appreciative Inquiry to Understand the Perspectives of High School Mathematics Teachers — 75
James M. Meneguzzo

Chapter 6: Lessons Learned About Job-Embedded Learning 91
Sally J. Zepeda

Index 105

About the Editor 111

About the Contributors 113

Series Editor's Introduction

Why a new book series on school leadership, and what does this particular series have to offer among the many fine books already published in the field of school and educational leadership?

Research over the past decade has confirmed what many educators, policy makers, think tanks, and others viscerally knew: leadership makes a difference for a host of dependent variables, including the most important one, student achievement. Additional research is needed, however, to more fully refine and uncover how, in fact, school leaders make a difference in a host of other areas. The answers to additional research questions will offer further legitimacy and draw greater attention to the field of educational leadership. The questions (which can possibly prompt potential authors to submit a book proposal) include the following, among others:

What does continuing increased accountability and high-stakes testing have on teacher morale, principal self-efficacy, and student achievement?
What additional information do we need about systems thinking and its relationship to school leadership?
What are the specific gender differences as related to leading schools?
What is the precise role played by school leaders in fostering inclusive educational practices?
How is social justice best fostered by school leaders?
What specific educational leadership strategies reduce the black/white achievement gap?
How might school leaders implement an effective, data-driven decision-making process in their schools?
What are the critical factors affecting high performance among principals?
What is the role of school leaders in reducing school violence?

How do leadership practices positively influence school-community partnerships?

What is the association between transformational leadership and teacher self-efficacy?

How does shared leadership affect school morale and productivity?

How do various types or forms of leadership impact organizational effectiveness?

What are the social, cultural, political and historical factors that influence the practice of educational leadership in different countries?

How do leadership practices differ in differing contexts, social, cultural or otherwise?

What are the theoretical and practical differences among educational administration, management, and leadership?

Why is an international perspective so critical for better understanding the challenges of leading schools in the 21st century?

How can school leaders address race and identity, bias and privilege, and racialized current events?

How can comparative research studies help us better understand educational leadership?

What can we learn from studying educational leaders beyond the school level (e.g., district and board [or ministry] of education leaders)?

To what extent does emotional labor impact educational leaders?

How can principals encourage action research and other alternatives to supervision to enhance teacher professional growth?

How do school leaders effectively implement new technologies not just for the sake of technology but to deepen learning and provide better support for teachers?

What are the consequences of workload on the effectiveness of school leaders?

What are the challenges that school leaders face in differing regional contexts?

How do school leaders develop the skills and knowledge they need to understand teachers' and students' needs and effectively guide learning?

How do effective school leaders balance administrative duties with instructional priorities?

What new educational management strategies can help teachers better confront classroom behavioral issues?

How do school leaders coordinate curriculum and instructional initiatives across schools?

Given time and budget constraints, how can school leaders find the resources to support an artful education (music, dance, creative writing, etc.) for all students?

How do increased efforts to promote teacher leadership impact the work of principals and their assistants?
What new innovative ideas can principals implement to deal with the increasingly complex landscape of curriculum today?
How can principals support teacher-led professional development?
What is the role of identity in fostering principal self-efficacy?
How can school leaders help schools become more integral to their surrounding communities—and how can they better leverage community resources and connections to support their students and teachers?
How can we better balance interest and work in instructional leadership with other important leadership responsibilities?
How can districts support assistant principals and prepare new principals as they take the helm of the school?
How do we induct and sustain good principals?
How can we best prepare future school leaders?

Most fundamentally, the Rowman & Littlefield School Leadership Series is premised on a need to connect theory to practice. Each of these questions relies on a sound theoretical base that has important, if not critical, relevance to the world of practice. This international series, in other words, reflects cutting-edge theories and practices in school leadership that attempt to bridge the perennial divide between theory and practice.

Although we try to publish manuscripts that have relevance to an international audience, we will accept more localized research that might only be applicable in a specific context. The manuscript, of course, must meet the rigors of academic research and have significant impact on practice. Feel free to query the series editor.

The series motto is modeled after Kurt Lewin's famous statement, and I paraphrase, that there is no sound theory without practice, and no good practice that is not based on theory. Authors are expected to illustrate the intimate and integral connection between these two divides. In this respect, we are unique because we do not accept proposals that are "heavy" on one side or the other; rather, we look for manuscripts that are intellectually engaging and have a sound theoretical base yet are firmly grounded in the daily lives of school leaders. I welcome readers to join this effort to increase knowledge in our field and affect daily school practice by submitting a proposal on any of the topics mentioned previously, or any other relevant ones. Feel free to communicate with the series editor at yosglanz@gmail.com.

As series editor, I would like to take this opportunity to thank my advisory board, listed below, for their efforts in seeing the series to fruition. Their feedback to the authors and the editor were instrumental in crafting a well-researched, practical, and readable volume.

Yin Cheong Cheng, Education University of Hong Kong—Tai Po, Hong Kong
Brent Davies, University of Hull—Hull, United Kingdom
Francis M. Duffy, Gallaudet University—Washington, DC, United States
Helen M. Hazi, West Virginia University at Morgantown—West Virginia, United States
Alfredo Ramirez Jr., Texas A&M International University—Texas, United States
Chen Schechter, Bar Ilan University—Ramant Gan, Israel
Karen Seashore Louis, University of Minnesota—Minnesota, United States
Lyn Sharratt, OISE, University of Toronto—Toronto, Canada
Duncan Waite, Texas State University—Texas, United States
Jane Wilkinson, Monash University—Victoria, Australia

Special acknowledgment is also extended to Tom Koerner (vice president and publisher for education issues), Carlie Wall (managing editor), and Emily Tuttle (assistant editor) for their support. Special thanks to Sue Canavan of the former Christopher-Gordon Publishers for first shepherding the idea for this series. I hope this volume and the series will receive wide acknowledgment for making a difference in the field of educational leadership.

Volume Introduction

As series editor, I am excited to introduce the first volume of the Rowman & Littlefield School Leadership Series, Sally J. Zepeda's *Making Learning Job-Embedded: Cases from the Field of Instructional Leadership*. I could not have wished for a more appropriate text to initiate the R&L School Leadership Series. Sally Zepeda's edited book is an excellent example of our goal to connect theory with practice. The volume offers a collection of powerful chapters focusing on the role of instructional leaders in helping teachers acquire the knowledge and skills needed for effective teaching by embedding that learning in their work. The book, as a whole, will offer instructional leaders with valuable insights on how to engage teachers in job-embedded learning, based on sound educational theory.

Although this book is not primarily focused in the international context, I think its ideas are indeed relevant to schools all over the world. Job-embedded learning, especially in terms of teacher professional development, can raise important questions for educational leaders in a variety of contexts. All readers, regardless of context, need to ask themselves these, among other, questions: What learning opportunities count as being job embedded? How might job-embedded professional development, for example, improve teaching and student learning outcomes? What does research, in the international arena, say about job-embedded learning? How can schools, anywhere, implement job-embedded learning properly? How might we best assess job-embedded learning's effectiveness in achieving stated objectives?

Professor Zepeda, among the most prolific scholars in our field today, has brilliantly assembled the work of a group of her doctoral students to provide readers with a glimpse into important research efforts. Each chapter is richly detailed, relevant, interesting, and well written. The authors are conversant with the literature and ground their work in real cases from the field. These four studies examine professional learning broadly and address critical questions such as: How are school leaders able to draw upon extant research to provide coherent, relevant, and meaningful learning opportunities for teachers? These chapters also address fundamental questions such as: What have teachers learned from their work in job-embedded contexts and experiences?

I am without doubt that Professor Zepeda's work here will find a receptive audience because of the educational climate we face in terms of pressure to raise academic achievement among all students and the need to attract and hire the highest qualified teachers. *Making Learning Job-Embedded: Cases from the Field of Instructional Leadership* is an important contribution to our field and on behalf of the advisory board, I thank Professor Zepeda and her committed and talented contributors for a work that will certainly make its mark.

Jeffrey Glanz
November 23, 2017

Preface

Making Learning Job-Embedded: Cases from the Field of Instructional Leadership is a book for sitting principals and assistant principals aspiring to the principalship. Teacher leaders, regardless of role (e.g., lead teacher, mentor, department chair) can gain insights from the case studies presented in this book. The cases in this edited volume serve as a reminder that practice and research can be mutually informed through purposeful efforts to learn lessons from each. The synergy between practice and research was a motivator to bring this collection of work to print.

This book is important for three interrelated reasons. First, the chapters examine very specific aspects of professions learning that school leaders need to understand to be able to create systems that support teachers as they teach students, interact with colleagues, participate in team meetings, and carry out so many of the other responsibilities that constitute the work of being a teacher.

Second, with many teacher evaluation systems including professional learning as a mandatory component, school leaders must be able to bring coherence to instructional supervision and teacher evaluation by exploring, for example, how job-embedded learning can support teacher growth and development and how school-wide programs can nurture teachers from the very newest to the veteran. School leaders are in a position to nurture a learning culture that fosters agency for teachers and encourages them to take an active lead in learning alongside their peers.

Third, this book illustrates how misaligned goals can dampen learning for teachers by emphasizing that our view of teachers as professionals can go a long way in the identification, design, and implementation of job-embedded learning opportunities for teachers. Without such efforts, professional development will continue to be the butt of jokes with the punch line *useless*. For school leaders, it's more than having an interest in professional learning—it's recognizing our need to ensure that teachers are learning from their work, every day.

Each chapter of this book is based on dissertation research conducted in schools that were representative of the variance found in preK–12 schools regardless of location and in urban, suburban, and rural contexts. The chapter authors bring credibility as they serve in such roles as instructional coach, assistant principal, central office leader, and other closely related positions that prepare teachers and examine policies related to professional learning. The authors are strong proponents of job-embedded learning, and from their research, rich portrayals of job-embedded learning emerge.

Acknowledgments

There are many people who worked behind the scenes to support this effort. From the University of Georgia, two research assistants Phillip D. Grant and Sevda Yildirim—both working on their doctor of philosophy degrees in the Department of Educational Administration and Policy—assisted with critical tasks to ensure deadlines were met.

A special thank you is extended to Dr. Tom Koerner, vice president and publisher for education issues at Rowman & Littlefield, and to Emily Tuttle, assistant editor, and Carlie Wall, managing editor, who left no detail to chance. Also appreciated are the efforts of Emily Eastridge, Editorial Assistant, and Lisa Whittington, Production Editor, who worked behind the scenes in production at Rowman & Littlefield to get this book ready to print. I am deeply indebted to Dr. Jeffrey Glanz, series editor, for his leadership and his encouragement to move forward with this project. Jeffrey, thank you for tapping into the work I am doing here at the University of Georgia to carry forward the torch of professional learning, supervision, and leadership that supports these areas in preK–12 schools.

To the chapter authors, without your dedication to the profession, this book would not have been possible. It is with great pride that I present your individual works and this collective achievement that promises to support the efforts of teachers, leaders, and the schools in which job-embedded learning can make a difference. You are the difference-makers!

Introduction

This book offers the foundations of professional and job-embedded learning. The chapters can be read in any order based on the reader's interest. By reviewing the table of contents, the reader will find a wide range of areas related to professional and job-embedded learning at the elementary, middle, and high school levels in preK–12 schools.

To support readability, all the chapters include key sections:

- a scenario;
- a highlight of the key ideas within the chapter;
- an abstract;
- an overview of the key literature related to the study;
- a discussion of the context of the study;
- a brief review of the research methods;
- a presentation of the findings;
- a discussion of the findings; and then,
- a presentation of the implications of these findings for school leaders.

Each chapter then ends with discussion questions and suggested readings to support ongoing reflection and conversations about professional learning, followed by pertinent references.

OVERVIEW OF THE CHAPTERS

Chapter 1, *Getting to Job-Embedded Learning*, gives us a general survey of job-embedded learning and professional learning.

In Chapter 2, *Understanding the Job-Embedded Learning Experiences of Middle School Teachers*, Brandi Wade Worsham examines how a group of suburban middle school teachers constructed understandings of their job-embedded learning experiences and how they made sense of informal and formal learning during the day. Sensemaking theory is used as a construct to understand better how teachers interpret and implement in their classrooms knowledge and skills gained from job-embedded learning opportunities.

Chapter 3, *Creating Coherence Between Teacher Evaluation and Ongoing Teacher Learning by Engaging in Collegial Goal Groups*, features an examination by Jen Cole of the perceptions of elementary school teachers in an urban setting. She examines the individual professional goals of teachers in a collegial group setting as a form of job-embedded professional learning. Through the synergy of goal groups, Cole found that the participants more readily engaged in risk-taking, increased their individual and collective capacity for learning, and accelerated the diffusion of instructional knowledge within and beyond the structures of the groups.

In Chapter 4, *The Impact of Incoherent Professional Learning onStandards-Based Reform*, Michael P. Cassidy examines urban middle school science teachers' perspectives of their professional development targeting Common Core State Standards for literacy in science. His findings revealed that teachers received inconsistent professional learning, the activities associated with professional learning were based on Next Gen Science Standards not adopted by the school district, and the teachers were exposed to inapplicable instructional strategies. By the end of the year, the teachers reported a lack of knowledge about the standards and how these standards were to be covered in their classrooms.

The following chapter, Chapter 5, *Professional Development: Using Appreciative Inquiry to Understand the Perspectives of High School Mathematics Teachers*, features an examination by James M. Meneguzzo of the perspectives of nine high school mathematics teachers in a rural setting. Using appreciative inquiry methods, the teachers were engaged to identify their professional development needs and the key factors of successful professional development that led to improvements in instructional practices. Participants highlighted relevance, content specificity, modeling, reflection, and feedback as essential for effective professional development. Each participant also expressed in his or her own way this sentiment: Just ask us what we need because we are professionals.

Finally, in Chapter 6, *Lessons Learned About Job-Embedded Learning*, I discuss themes running through the preceding chapters and their implications for school and system leaders.

Chapter 1

Getting to Job-Embedded Learning

Sally J. Zepeda

KEY IDEAS IN THIS CHAPTER

- Professional learning
- Job-embedded learning
- Overview of the book

INTRODUCTION

The call for high-quality, professional learning embedded daily for every teacher must be answered. The research and literature related to professional learning all point to its necessity and the inherent processes that add value for adult learners (Darling-Hammond, Hyler, & Gardner, 2017; Desimone, 2009, 2011). However, the reality is that practices in the field often do not align with the principles of high-quality, professional learning that engages teachers in opportunities to learn from the work they do in their classrooms (Zepeda, 2015).

Professional learning for teachers has been put on hold with quick fixes to shore up deficiencies often created as an outcome of high-stakes reform efforts that mandate swift action related to what gets taught and how. Quick fixes merely patch weak systems. The quick-fix model of professional learning is costly.

In *The Mirage: Confronting the Hard Truth About Our Quest for Teacher Development*, it is reported by systems included in the study that the average spending for professional learning was "between 6 and 9 percent of their annual budgets, or an average of $18,000 per teacher, per year" (New Teacher

Project, 2015, p. 10). These numbers are consistent with a joint report from Learning Forward (2017) and the National Commission on Teaching & America's Future that indicates 2.6 billion dollars are dispersed from federal monies annually to school systems that often spend an additional $12,000 per teacher per year from their own funds for professional learning (Calvert, 2016).

When teachers learn from their work, students benefit from these efforts. However, school leaders must actively support systems within their schools that nurture learning for teachers. Research consistently indicates that the effects of teachers on student learning are immense; therefore, leaders must with a sense of urgency provide teachers multiple opportunities to work together so they can learn from each other not only by studying their peers' practices but also from the insights, feedback, and discourse that occur when teachers collaborate.

This volume includes four studies that describe and detail findings from dissertation research conducted by scholar-practitioners in preK–12 schools. These studies examined broadly professional learning—how teachers learned from their work and how they grew in their understandings of their work and interactions with others. Conclusions and recommendations are offered for school leaders to support an environment that embraces job-embedded learning. The messages from within and across the chapters point to the primacy of teacher engagement and the value of job-embedded learning.

This chapter frames the purposes and intents of professional learning and the construct of job-embedded learning as highly personalized opportunities for adults to grow. The chapter then ends with a broad overview of each of the following chapters.

PROFESSIONAL LEARNING

Professional learning is understood first by identifying what it is not. From there, the concepts about professional learning are examined.

What Professional Learning Is Not

Let's first get to some ideas about what professional learning is not. Professional learning is not a deficit approach for working with teachers (Zepeda, 2006, 2015); professional learning is not a "fix-it" program (Zepeda, 2012); and professional learning is not a remediation plan (Zepeda, 2016, 2017). Through deficit approaches, professional development is highly prescriptive with mindless, step-by-step solutions that position teachers as receivers of information not necessarily related to their own needs—and more than likely far removed from the needs of students.

What Professional Learning Is

Desimone (2011) defines professional learning as "a complex array of interrelated learning opportunities" (p. 69). "Effective professional development is intensive, ongoing, and connected to practice; focused on student learning and teaching specific curriculum content; and aligned with school improvement priorities and goals," according to the policy position of Learning Forward (2017) in support of continued Title I funding legislated in the Every Student Succeeds Act of 2015 (2017, n.p.).

The Every Student Succeeds Act of 2015 (ESSA) includes purposeful language: "The term 'professional development' means activities that . . . are sustained (not stand-alone, 1-day, or short-term workshops), intensive, collaborative, job-embedded, data-driven, and classroom focused" (SEC. 1177, Section 8002, pp. 295–296, para., 42). ESSA sends a strong message in its definition and descriptions for professional learning that

1. Enables students to learn;
2. Supports teachers to meet the challenges of state academic standards;
3. Calls for "personalized plans" of professional learning for teachers based on "observation or other feedback";
4. Uses data to inform professional development for teachers; and
5. Creates mechanisms to follow-up on professional development.

Professional learning is supported by key research as illustrated in Table 1.1.

In summary, high-quality, professional development should be ongoing, intense, content-focused, and aligned to state and district goals (Yoon, Duncan, Lee, Scarloss, & Shapley, 2007) as well as designed in ways that provide coherence for adult learners in schools and their systems (Desimone, 2009, 2011). Job-embedded learning is foundational to professional learning for adults.

JOB-EMBEDDED LEARNING

The principles of adult learning provide a foundation for job-embedded professional development. Hunzicker (2011) offers a succinct synthesis of teachers as adult learners:

Table 1.1 Key Research on Professional Learning

Darling-Hammond, Hyler, and Gardner (2017)	Desimone (2009) and Desimone and Garet (2015)
Professional development • is content focused; • incorporates active learning by utilizing adult learning theory; • supports collaboration, typically in job-embedded contexts; • uses models and modeling of effective practice; • provides coaching and expert support; • offers opportunities for feedback and reflection; and • is of sustained duration.	Professional learning includes core features that lead to learning • content focus, • active learning, • coherence, • duration, and • collective participation.

Adapted from **Effective Teacher Professional Development** by L. Darling-Hammond, M. E. Hyler, and M. Gardner, 2017, Palo Alto, CA: Learning Policy Institute; "Improving Impact Studies of Teachers' Professional Development: Toward Better Conceptualizations and Measures" by L. M. Desimone, 2009, **Educational Researcher, 38**(3), 181–199; and "Best Practices in Teachers' Professional Development in the United States" by L. M. Desimone and M. S. Garet, 2015, **Psychology, Society and Education, 7**(3), 252–263.

As a group, adult learners approach learning with clear goals in mind, using their life experiences to make sense of new information. They are motivated by opportunities to address problems—and create solutions—that relate directly to their lives. They prefer open-ended learning activities and function best when they have a voice in the direction and pace of their learning.

Therefore, effective professional development is anything that engages teachers in learning activities that are supportive, job-embedded, instructionally focused, collaborative, and ongoing. With these characteristics in place, teachers are more likely to consider professional development relevant and authentic, which makes teacher learning and improved teaching practice more likely (p. 177).

Darling-Hammond and McLaughlin (2011) underscore that principles of adult learning are an integral part of job-embedded environments where "teachers learn by doing, reading, and reflecting (just as students do); by collaborating with other teachers; by looking closely at students and their work; and by sharing what they see" (p. 83).

Job-Embedded Learning Defined

"Instructional leaders need to learn about the work of helping teachers [to] learn" (Breidenstein, Fahey, Glickman, & Hensley, 2012, p. 12), and a major way to engage teachers is to promote job-embedded learning as an integral part of the work day, every day, not just during pre-planning and system-days earmarked for professional development. Croft, Coggshall, Dolan, Powers, and Killion (2010) define job-embedded professional development as "teacher learning that is grounded in day-to-day teaching practice and is designed to enhance teachers' content-specific instructional practices with the intent of improving student learning" (p. 2).

Job-embedded learning means that professional development is a continuous thread that can be found throughout the culture of a school. Job-embedded learning is what occurs during a teacher's "daily work activities" (Wood & Killian, 1998, p. 52) that signals collaboration, joint problem-posing, problem-solving, and a sincere desire to improve practice from the lessons learned from teaching and interacting with peers (Zepeda, 2015). Parise and Spillane (2010) suggest that on-the-job learning opportunities include "interactions with colleagues around teaching and learning, including conversations about instruction, peer observations, feedback, and advice-seeking about instruction" (p. 324).

The Benefits of Job-Embedded Learning

There are numerous benefits associated with embedding learning in the daily work that teachers do to support student learning. From research and practice, job-embedded learning, in short,

- addresses the individual needs of teachers or teams of teachers (Hirsh, 2009);
- provides the opportunity to increase student achievement by improving teacher instructional practices (Borko, 2004);
- is sustained over time every work day (Tienken & Stonaker, 2007);
- promotes a cooperative approach to support the teacher as a researcher capable of inquiring into practices (Cochran-Smith & Lytle, 2009; Dana & Yendol-Hoppey, 2009);
- fosters collaboration and reflective practices (Feiman-Nemser, 2012);
- promotes active learning because teachers are able to observe one another teaching, co-develop lesson plans, engage in long-term discussions, give concrete feedback on practice, and analyze student work through artifacts and evidence (Desimone, 2011);
- focuses on the daily work of teachers and occurs in real time both in and out of the classroom (Zepeda, 2015);
- reduces the time between what is learned and its implementation and refinement in practice: in the classroom with students and with colleagues (von Frank, 2009);
- is personalized (edSurge, 2014); and

- includes processes that can generate feedback—for example, mentoring, peer coaching, study groups, videotape analysis of teaching, and journaling (Zepeda, 2012, 2015).

Job-embedded professional learning occurs throughout the day (Yoon et al., 2007; Tienken & Stonaker, 2007); is context specific to the school (Croft et al., 2010); is structured for active learning, collaboration, and applications that can be put to use in the classroom immediately (Penuel, Fishman, Yamaguchi, & Gallagher, 2007); and is based on data (Schnellert, Butler, & Higginson, 2008).

The Many Forms of Job-Embedded Learning

The forms of job-embedded learning are replete with opportunities for teachers to collaborate and learn from one another. Moreover, job-embedded learning opportunities support reflection, feedback on practice, and forms of action research and inquiry so that teachers can think about what they do in their classrooms to impact student learning. As web technologies evolve and as we learn more about how teachers learn from their practices, job-embedded learning opportunities, processes, and forms will shift to be more responsive to the needs of teachers. Table 1.2 offers examples of the forms that support job-embedded learning.

School context, the needs of teachers, the support of school leaders, the culture of the school, and the willingness of teachers to engage with one another all work to determine the types and forms of job-embedded learning and how opportunities evolve in schools. Job-embedded learning opportunities will continue to evolve as do the needs of teachers and the schools in which they work. Access and use of digital technologies and platforms will also continue to evolve and extend job-embedded learning opportunities where teachers can learn from one another and in communities that go beyond the boundaries of the schoolhouse.

The next section highlights the following chapters and serves as an open invitation to the reader to explore the possibilities of job-embedded learning and learn how leaders can support the efforts of teachers as they engage in the complex work of examining their classroom practices.

OVERVIEW OF THE BOOK

The chapter authors present findings of dissertation research that are based on the day-to-day life of schools and their systems. All the authors are graduates of the University of Georgia, and their dissertations are available online.

Table 1.2 Illustrative Forms of Collaborative Job-Embedded Professional Development

Forms of Job-Embedded Learning	Brief Description
Action Research	To find out what works in the classroom or to solve a problem of practice, teachers select an aspect of their work to investigate. This includes cycles of collecting, analyzing, and reflecting on the meaning of data, modifying practice, and then repeating the process.
Book Studies	Small groups of teachers read a book of interest related to some aspect of practice, meet to discuss, and then draw inferences about how the content of the book can support the improvement of practice. Typically, book studies are organized around a topic of interest; an area related to a school-wide, improvement-targeted goal; or an issue of practice at a grade level or with a subject-specific group of teachers. Conversations are at the heart of the book study as members share insights and ask questions of the text and each other to learn from the perspectives of other members.
Lesson Study	Following a cycle, teachers plan a lesson together, the lesson is taught with colleagues observing the lesson, and then teachers meet and discuss the strengths of the lesson, making suggestions for improvement. Sometimes the lesson is revised and presented again following the cycle.
Online Learning	Online learning communities using Twitter, Facebook, blogs, and other digital supports, regardless of when and where those supports are accessed, provide real-time, professional learning.
Peer Observations	Peer observations provide opportunities for teachers to observe one another at work through, for example, the "P.O.P Cycle": pre-observation conversation, classroom observation, and post-observation conversation. Peers provide feedback, encourage reflection, and support ongoing inquiry based on the focus of the classroom observation and the analysis of data.

Forms of Job-Embedded Learning	Brief Description
Portfolio	The portfolio is a tool to chronicle growth across time in a specific area. Teachers assemble lesson plans, student work, and other materials used directly in the classroom. Reflecting on artifacts is an integral part of the portfolio.
Study Groups	In small groups, teachers generate topics for study related to school improvement goals or instructional practices. Teachers examine student data, read educational literature, and engage in structured discussions to consider the implications for classroom practices.
Studying Student Work	Studying student work allows teachers to develop a common understanding of instruction as well as identify student misconceptions and evaluate teaching methods. By studying artifacts, teachers are better able to modify practice based on what is discovered about teaching through student work.
Whole-Faculty Study	An extended model of professional learning, whole-faculty study groups "mobilize" schools to action by putting student learning at the center of school improvement efforts. Whole-faculty study groups have an organizational focus, focusing on the primary goal of schools to increase student learning.

Adapted from *Professional Development: What Works* (2nd ed.) by S. J. Zepeda, 2012, New York, NY: Routledge; and *Job-Embedded Professional Development: Support, Collaboration, and Learning in Schools* by S. J. Zepeda, 2015, New York, NY: Routledge.

They examine professional learning that is embedded in the work lives of the participants that were part of these studies. These studies were conducted in elementary schools, middle schools, and high schools. The context of the schools includes rural, suburban, and urban settings.

In Chapter 2, *Understanding the Job-Embedded Learning Experiences of Middle School Teachers*, Brandi Wade Worsham investigates job-embedded learning experiences constructed, and experienced, by a group of five middle school teachers in a suburban school district that enrolls approximately 7,000 students. She examines (1) how teachers make sense of, and give meaning to, their job-embedded learning experiences that occur formally and informally throughout the school day; (2) how teachers' interpretations impact their implementation of newly acquired knowledge and skills; and (3) how school administrators can facilitate and maximize the learning experiences of teachers.

Case analysis results revealed that each study participant shared similarities and differences when constructing the meaning of job-embedded learning experiences in their schools. Five themes emerged centering on identity, motivation, reflection, collaboration, and application.

In Chapter 3, *Creating Coherence Between Supervision and Ongoing Teacher Learning*, Jen Cole examines elementary school teachers' perceptions of their individual professional goals in a collegial group setting as a form of job-embedded professional learning. The school system is an urban-like one that enrolls approximately 13,500 students. The school where this study took place enrolls about 450 students in kindergarten through fifth grade.

The study's five findings suggest that (1) teachers place high value on the collaborative process of goal groups regardless of barriers encountered; (2) professional teacher relationships positively influence the school culture; (3) a confluence of individual and collaborative work amplifies learning at both individual and group levels; (4) goal group professional learning is the anchor that links goals to professional learning and to evaluation; and (5) as teachers continue to engage in collaborative work, they bring lasting changes to their instructional practices as they change their beliefs about teaching.

In Chapter 4, *The Impact of Incoherent Professional Learning on Standards-Based Reform*, Michael P. Cassidy examines middle school science teachers' perspectives of their professional development targeting Common Core State Standards for literacy in science. The study took place in a Title I urban middle school that serves a population of nearly 700 students in grades 6 through 8.

The findings revealed that teachers lacked knowledge of standards, engaged in professional learning activities that were fragmented and incoherent, and were exposed to inapplicable instructional strategies. A lack of administrative support at the building level and the mixed messages given by the district created confusion for the teachers.

In Chapter 5, *Professional Development: Using Appreciative Inquiry to Understand the Perspectives of High School Mathematics Teachers*, James M. Meneguzzo examines the perspectives of nine high school mathematics teachers who were asked to (1) identify their professional development needs through the use of appreciative inquiry method, and (2) identify key factors to successful professional development leading to instructional practice improvement. The nine teachers worked in two of three rural high schools that served approximately 19,500 students who represented a diverse ethnic population and an equally diverse socioeconomic status.

The study's findings indicated that the participants' desired professional development, which offered hands-on activities, promoted follow-up and immediate feedback on implementation of learned strategies, provided opportunities for self-reflection and collaborative discussion with peers, and was geared toward their specific content areas in mathematics. The participants highlighted relevance, content specificity, modeling, reflection, and feedback as essential for effective professional development.

Chapter 6 offers an overall analysis of the above studies by focusing on the processes and nature of job-embedded professional learning. Lessons for school leaders are offered to extend thinking about ways to support teachers.

REFERENCES

Borko, H. (2004). Professional development and teacher learning: Mapping the terrain. *Educational Researcher*, *33*(8), 3–15. doi:10.3102/0013189X033008003

Breidenstein, A., Fahey, K., Glickman, C. D., & Hensley, F. (2012). *Leading for powerful learning: A guide for instructional leaders*. New York, NY: Teachers College Press.

Calvert, L. (2016). *Moving from compliance to agency: What teachers need to make professional learning work*. Oxford, OH: Learning Forward and NCTAF. Retrieved from https://nctaf.org/wp-content/uploads/2016/03/NCTAF-Learning-Forward_Moving-from-Compliance-to-Agency_What-Teachers-Need-to-Make-Professional-Learning-Work.pdf

Cochran-Smith, M., & Lytle, S. (2009). *Inquiry as stance: Practitioner research for the next generation*. New York, NY: Teachers College Press.

Croft, A., Coggshall, J. G., Dolan, M., Powers, E., & Killion, J. (2010). *Job-embedded professional development: What it is, who is responsible, and how to get it done well* [Issue brief]. Washington, DC: National Comprehensive Center for Teacher Quality.

Dana, N. F., & Yendol-Hoppey, D. (2009). *The reflective educator's guide to classroom research: Learning to teach and teaching to learn through practitioner inquiry*. Thousand Oaks, CA: Corwin.

Darling-Hammond, L., Hyler, M. E., & Gardner, M. (2017). *Effective teacher professional development*. Palo Alto, CA: Learning Policy Institute. Retrieved from https://webcache.googleusercontent.com/search?q=cache:hSYNgHwJx_AJ:https://learningpolicyinstitute.org/product/effective-teacher-professional-development-report+&cd=1&hl=en&ct=clnk&gl=us

Darling-Hammond, L., & McLaughlin, M. W. (2011). Policies that support professional development in an era of reform. *Phi Delta Kappan*, *92*(6), 81–92. Retrieved from http://pdkintl.org/publications/

Desimone, L. M. (2009). Improving impact studies of teachers' professional development: Toward better conceptualizations and measures. *Educational Researcher*, *38*(3), 181–199. doi:http://doi.org/10.3102/0013189X08331140

Desimone, L. M. (2011). A primer on professional development. *Phi Delta Kappan*, *92*(6), 68–71. Retrieved from http://doi.org/10.2307/25822820

Desimone, L. M., & Garet, M. S. (2015). Best practices in teachers' professional development in the United States. *Psychology, Society and Education*, *7*(3), 252–263. Retrieved from www.psye.com

edSurge. (2014). How districts get personal: Retooling professional development. Burlington, CA: edSurge. Retrieved from https://www.edsurge.com/research/guides/from-pre-fab-to-personalized-how-districts-are-retooling-professional-development

Every Student Succeeds Act, Pub. L. 114–95, 129 Stat. 1802 (2015).

Feiman-Nemser, S. (2012). *Teachers as learners*. Cambridge, MA: Harvard Education Press.

Hirsh, S. (2009). A new definition. *Journal of Staff Development*, *30*(4), 10–16. Retrieved from https://learningforward.org/publications/jsd

Hunzicker, J. (2011). Effective professional development for teachers: A checklist. *Professional Development in Education*, *37*(2), 177–179. doi:10.1080/19415257.2010.523955.

Learning Forward (2017). *Title IIA: Supporting effective instruction state grants program. Critical support for teaching and leading: Call to action*. Oxford, OH: Learning Forward. Author. Retrieved from https://learningforward.org/docs/default-source/getinvolved/title-ii-one-pager-060817.pdf?sfvrsn=2

New Teacher Project (2015). *The mirage: Confronting the hard truth about our quest for teacher development*. Washington, DC: TNTP. Author. Retrieved from http://tntp.org/publications/view/the-mirage-confronting-the-truth-about-our-quest-for-teacher-development

Parise, L. M., & Spillane, J. P. (2010). Teacher learning and instructional change: How formal and on-the-job learning opportunities predict changes in elementary school teachers' instructional practice. *Elementary School Journal*, *110*(3), 323–346. doi:10.1086/648981

Penuel, W. R., Fishman, B. J., Yamaguchi, R., & Gallagher, L. P. (2007). What makes professional development effective? Strategies that foster curriculum implementation. *American Educational Research Journal*, *44*(4), 921–958. doi:10.3102/0002831207308221

Schnellert, L. M., Butler, D. L., & Higginson, S. K. (2008). Co-constructors of data, co-constructors of meaning: Teacher professional development in an age of accountability. *Teaching and Teacher Education: An International Journal of Research and Studies*, *24*(3), 725–750. https://doi.org/10.1016/j.tate.2007.04.001

Tienken, C. H., & Stonaker, L. (2007). When every day is professional development day. *Journal of Staff Development*, *28*(2), 24–29. Retrieved from https://learningforward.org/publications/jsd/page/3

von Frank, V. (2009). Ambassadors of learning: Teachers' enthusiasm builds momentum for district's long-running program. *Journal of Staff Development*, *30*(2), 24–30. Retrieved from https://learningforward.org/publications/jsd/page/3

Wood, F. H., & Killian, J. E. (1998). Job-embedded learning makes the difference in school improvement. *Journal of Staff Development, 19*(1), 52–54. Retrieved from https://learningforward.org/publications/jsd

Yoon, K. S., Duncan, T., Lee, S. W.-Y., Scarloss, B., & Shapley, K. L. (2007). *Reviewing the evidence on how teacher professional development affects student achievement* (Issues & Answers Report, REL 2007–No. 033). Washington, DC: U.S. Department of Education, Institute of Education Sciences, National Center for Education Evaluation and Regional Assistance, Regional Educational Laboratory Southwest. Retrieved from http://ies.ed.gov/ncee/edlabs

Zepeda, S. J. (2006). High stakes supervision: We must do more. *International Journal of Leadership in Education, 9*(1), 61–73. doi:10.1080/13603120500448154

Zepeda, S. J. (2012). *Professional development: What works* (2nd ed.). New York, NY: Routledge.

Zepeda, S. J. (2015). *Job-embedded professional development: Support, collaboration, and learning in schools*. New York, NY: Routledge.

Zepeda, S. J. (2016). Principals' perspectives: Professional learning and marginal teachers on formal plans of improvement. *Research in Educational Administration & Leadership, 1*(1), 25–59. Retrieved from http://dergipark.ulakbim.gov.tr/eyla/index

Zepeda, S. J. (2017). *Instructional supervision: Applying tools and concepts* (4th ed.). New York, NY: Routledge.

Chapter 2

Understanding the Job-Embedded Learning Experiences of Middle School Teachers

Brandi Wade Worsham

SCENARIO

Mrs. Jones and Mr. King often visit one another's classroom during their morning planning time to discuss their teaching. On this day, Mrs. Jones shares her frustration regarding a lesson she taught about the order of operations to her first-period class. She tells Mr. King that her students seemed not to understand the concept and were reluctant to try problems independently. He offers her several suggestions for re-teaching the concept and ideas for motivating her students in her first period to take risks without consequences. Additionally, the pair discuss ways in which Mrs. Jones might modify her lesson for subsequent periods that day should they also experience similar difficulties. Before parting, Mrs. Jones and Mr. King agree to check in with each other at the end of the day to reflect on the success of the lesson.

KEY IDEAS IN THIS CHAPTER

- Effective professional development is ongoing, embedded, coherent, and collaborative.
- Job-embedded learning that resides in the daily practice of teachers facilitates the refinement and renewal of knowledge, skills, and teaching practices.
- Teachers' sensemaking is central to teacher negotiation, co-construction, and interpretation of job-embedded learning experiences.

ABSTRACT

This chapter examines how a group of middle school teachers construct understandings of their job-embedded learning experiences. Specifically, the chapter explores (1) how teachers make sense of and give meaning to informal and formal learning that occur during a school day, (2) how teachers' sensemaking influences their interpretation and implementation of learned knowledge and skills, and (3) how the learning experiences of teachers can be facilitated and supported by school leaders.

INTRODUCTION

Professional learning has the power to transform schools, improve teacher quality, and increase student achievement (Darling-Hammond, Wei, Andree, Richardson, & Orphanos, 2009). When teachers' knowledge, skills, and teaching practices are enhanced through embedded, relevant, and ongoing professional learning, the needs of teachers and students are more effectively evaluated and addressed. However, most professional development occurs through traditional, one-stop workshops in which minimal opportunities exist for teachers to collaborate, plan, and put into practice new knowledge and skills.

The importance of implementation of professional learning warrants a greater emphasis on how teachers make sense of and give meaning to their learning experiences within their work context. This study examines how middle school teachers construct understandings of their job-embedded learning experiences as they engage in the work of being a teacher.

OVERVIEW OF THE LITERATURE

The literature on professional development, job-embedded learning, professional development in the middle school, and sensemaking is presented to provide a context.

Professional Development

Collectively, scholars agree on several key features of effective professional development, including focus on content, emphasis on active learning, attention to coherence, consideration of duration, and the encouragement of collective participation (Guskey & Yoon, 2009; Hunzicker, 2011; Wei,

Darling-Hammond, & Adamson, 2010; Zepeda, 2017). Understanding the key features that make professional development effective is essential to improving student learning and teacher practice. Furthermore, a focus on effective professional development increases the transfer of new knowledge and skills and encourages refinement of existing teaching methods.

In addition, the relationship between effective professional development, teacher quality, and adult learning is worth examination. Professional development that incorporates hands-on activities (Glickman, Gordon, & Ross-Gordon, 2009), meets the perceived needs of the teacher (Zepeda, 2015), is learning centered (Coggshall, Rasmussen, Colton, Milton, & Jacques, 2012), and has a positive impact on teacher learning promotes teacher quality.

Additional factors, such as leadership, resources, organizational arrangements, and school climate and culture may contribute to the effectiveness of professional development and teacher learning; however, the situational nature of professional learning cannot be ignored (Gulamhussein, 2013; National Institute for Excellence in Teaching, 2012). Thus, opportunities for job-embedded learning offer a viable way for teachers to refine their teaching practice within the context and culture of their schools while still underscoring the key features of effective professional development.

Job-Embedded Learning

Job-embedded, or on-the-job, learning is learning that occurs by doing, by reflecting on experiences, and by generating and sharing new ideas with others (Wood & McQuarrie, 1999). It is grounded in the daily practice of teachers and presents a way to facilitate continuous formal and informal professional learning within the context of the teaching environment. Moreover, job-embedded learning aligns with and connects teacher learning to practice, focuses on student learning, and encompasses the key features of effective professional development (Coggshall et al., 2012; Guskey, 2014). Hence, job-embedded learning is a viable way to refine and renew teachers' knowledge and skills within their existing teaching practices.

Job-embedded learning typically occurs informally; however, formal opportunities that are planned, structured, and focused on a predefined topic or purpose exist (Ginsberg & Wlodkowski, 2010). Formal learning experiences might include classroom walk-throughs, book studies, lesson studies, learning circles, peer coaching, and other planned collaborative opportunities.

Conversely, informal learning experiences can occur anywhere and at any time, and these experiences are minimally structured and continuous learning opportunities that result from spontaneous interaction and collaboration (Ginsberg & Wlodkowski, 2010). Examples include impromptu conversations and interactions generated from mentoring, lesson reflection, collaborative check-ins, and hallway chats.

Given the situated nature of job-embedded learning, there are several essential conditions and attributes necessary for successful implementation. First, the learning experiences should adhere to adult learning principles, rely on collaboration and interaction, occur within the context of the school, and be supported by sufficient resources (Darling-Hammond & McLaughlin, 2011). Because job-embedded learning is relevant to teachers, it encourages reflection, includes feedback, promotes collaboration, and supports the transfer of new knowledge and skills to practice (Zepeda, 2017).

Job-embedded learning combats isolation, decreases the amount of time spent away from the job, and typically costs less. Finally, job-embedded learning provides multiple opportunities for teachers and administrators to document teacher reflection, collaboration, and performance (Coggshall et al., 2012).

Professional Development in the Middle School

Effective professional development at the middle school level is ongoing, focused on student outcomes, aligned with standards, and embedded in the work of teachers (Jackson & Davis, 2000; National Middle School Association, 2010). Pate and Thompson (2003) provide a list of recommendations for effective professional development in the middle school. The recommendations include a focus on content, active learning, and ongoing support; encourage collective participation; and align with federal, state, and local expectations.

Sensemaking

Sensemaking is a process of interpretation and meaning making that negotiates and co-constructs new knowledge based on the influences of one's environment and interactions with others (Weick, 2012). Sensemaking occurs when one uses prior knowledge and understanding to discover and apply new knowledge and experience. Therefore, sensemaking is both an individual and a collective process of constant negotiation that ties an individual's actions to that individual's worldview, understandings, and beliefs.

Most of the research on sensemaking is focused on interpretation and implementation of education policy (Coburn, 2005; Coburn & Woulfin, 2012), and sensemaking within the context of professional development is a relatively new area of inquiry (Colestock & Sherin, 2009). The scope of research on sensemaking and job-embedded learning is limited; therefore, this study contributes to the literature by examining how middle school teachers make sense of and give meaning to their job-embedded learning experiences.

CONTEXT OF THE STUDY AND RESEARCH METHODS

This study took place at North Willow Middle School (NWMS), a suburban public middle school in an eastern state. NWMS is one of three middle schools, and one of 14 schools in the district that serves predominately white, middle-class students; however, the demographics of the district are more diverse. NWMS is considered one of the highest performing middle schools in the region according to characteristics outlined in *This We Believe: Keys to Educating Young Adolescents* (National Middle School Association, 2010) and state statistical data.

Four middle school teachers participated in the study. Collectively, the participants were female, held advanced degrees, and had six to 29 years teaching experience. Two of the participants taught sixth grade and two taught seventh grade. Participants taught a combination of language arts/reading, science, and social studies. This study examines how the teachers made sense of and gave meaning to their job-embedded learning experiences.

A multicase study design helped explore the processes, perspectives, and experiences of the four middle school teachers as they learned during the school day while engaging in the work of being a teacher. A multicase study design enables researchers to document multiple perspectives and interactions, explore processes of change, and experience how sociocultural contexts influence the perspectives, interactions, and processes of individuals and groups (Yin, 2009). A multicase study design is appropriate for this study since it emphasizes the influence of context and culture on how teachers understand and interpret their job-embedded learning experiences.

Sensemaking theory is used to unpack teacher knowledge construction. Sensemaking theory assumes knowledge is co-constructed from action and interpretation within the context and culture of a specific environment (Choo, 2006). Sensemaking offers a way to organize and assign meaning to experiences (Weick, 2012) and is essential to understanding how teachers understand, interpret, and adapt new knowledge given their existing worldview and teaching practice (Coburn, 2005). Thus, sensemaking theory guides the collection, analysis, and interpretation of the data in this study.

Data were collected via interviews, shadowing, and learning logs. Initially, each participant was interviewed to gather data about her worldview, beliefs about professional development, and experiences with job-embedded learning. This information provided a foundation for understanding each participant's sensemaking. Next, each participant was shadowed for one school day as she engaged in job-embedded learning experiences. A field journal focused on the talk and actions of each participant was used to record how each teacher interacted and co-constructed meaning.

Finally, weekly learning logs were collected over a four-week period to document each participant's formal and informal job-embedded learning experiences. Participants were given prompts to help facilitate reflection; however, the participant determined what and how often to write. Follow-up emails were sent weekly by the researcher to further probe each participant's sensemaking of her learning experiences.

Within-case and cross-case analysis was used to examine data because this method allowed for the analysis of data from each teacher as a single case before collectively considering the commonalities among all the teachers represented as one case (Creswell, 2007). The constant comparative method (Glaser & Strauss, 1967) guided collecting, coding, and analyzing data from the interviews, shadowing, and learning logs of each participant as well as the collective group. Themes from the data were culled by using axial coding to see and then understand the relationship between and among codes and categories generated within and across the data (Corbin & Strauss, 2008).

FINDINGS

First, within-case analysis is presented. Each participant represents one case within the multicase study design. A summary of the sensemaking of each participant follows.

Case 1: Amanda

Amanda is a seventh-grade language arts/reading teacher with 18 years of teaching experience and four years of experience at her current school. Amanda's worldview and beliefs about teaching and learning are influenced by the schools she has taught in, including inner-city schools—with many students living in poverty and receiving English as a Second Language services—and affluent suburbs. She contends her prior teaching experiences have helped to shape her sensemaking of job-embedded learning by requiring her to identify what her students need to be successful in the classroom and then to develop a plan to ensure that she has the knowledge and skills to implement strategies and techniques.

During her initial interview, Amanda defined job-embedded learning as on-the-job training that occurs during the school day for the betterment of teaching. However, she noted that she does a lot of independent study outside school and brings those ideas into the classroom. She wondered if job-embedded learning must occur within the confines of the school day or if any learning experienced by a teacher that influences her teaching practice should encompass job-embedded learning.

Regardless of her uncertainty, Amanda reflects on several job-embedded learning opportunities in her learning logs, including content, grade-level, and leadership meetings; informal collaborative meetings and hallway check-ins; and book study group meetings. Specifically, she finds value in all her job-embedded learning experiences because each provides her with relevant information; however, the meaningfulness of such information is influenced by the delivery, relevance, and applicability of the content discussed. Learning experiences that are collaborative, relevant to her classroom, and afford her the opportunity to apply new content or instructional knowledge are preferred.

Case 2: Sarah

Sarah is a sixth-grade science and social studies teacher with 24 years of teaching experience and one year of experience at her current school. Like many of her colleagues, Sarah's prior teaching experience shapes her worldview and beliefs about teaching and learning. She has taught fourth through eighth grade, with 11 years in a neighboring district and 13 years in her current district. Sarah is vocal about her beliefs and opinions when speaking with her fellow teachers but reserved when speaking with administrators. Nonetheless, she continuously advocates for her students both in and out of the classroom. Her desire to ensure student success no doubt influences her sensemaking of the learning experiences she engages in during the school day.

Sarah's initial interview reveals the impact job-embedded learning can have on teachers. For instance, she defines job-embedded learning as learning from people you work with during the hours you are at work. Her understanding of the definition highlights the importance of collegial relationships as teachers work to improve and refine their teaching practice.

The learning logs submitted by Sarah prove insightful as she reflects on her job-embedded learning experiences, including content meetings, administrator and academic coach observations and feedback, and digital learning modules provided as a resource by the state department of education. In her learning logs, Sarah underscores the importance of collaborative meetings and she documents how her interactions with other colleagues help refine her existing teaching practice.

Sarah explains that her colleagues challenge her to think about the needs of her students when she is planning lessons and activities to meet content and student expectations. Going deeper into sensemaking, Sarah examines the fit between her teaching identity and philosophy in relation to what she actually implements after her own learning in the classroom.

Case 3: Leslie

Leslie is a seventh-grade social studies teacher with 29 years of teaching experience and 14 years of experience at her current school. Before her tenure in her current position, Leslie taught fifth grade in a rural, impoverished school for one year as well as sixth-grade social studies, language arts, and mathematics in an inner-city, metro area for 14 years. She describes herself as an innovative teacher who never does the same lesson twice. She dedicates a lot of time to learning about her students' needs and staying current with content and instructional strategies.

Leslie defines job-embedded learning as what you learn from your students, your colleagues, and your own independent study. She also explains that job-embedded learning is rooted in one's work environment and contingent on collegial relationships. In other words, how one makes sense of and gives meaning to a learning experience is dependent on the culture and context of the experience as well as interactions with and the influences of one's peers.

Leslie's learning logs provide several examples of job-embedded learning, such as book studies, collegial observations and feedback, peer mentoring, grade-level or leadership meetings, content workshops, conferences, and impromptu hallway conversations and check-ins. In one instance, Leslie chronicles her time mentoring a student teacher. She compares her teaching experience to the expectations and requirements of her student teacher. She finds meaning and value not only in preparing a future teacher but also in using that mentorship to reflect on and refine her teaching practice.

In a second example, Leslie details how powerful impromptu hallway conversations and check-ins can be during the school day. She recalls how disappointed she was that her students did not perform well on a test. She briefly chatted with a fellow teammate during class change about the results and then "on the fly" devised a plan for remediation and ideas for preventing similar results with her upcoming classes.

Case 4: Emily

Emily is a sixth-grade language arts/reading teacher with 19 years of teaching experience and one year of experience at her current school. To Emily, job-embedded learning occurs within the context of the school day and is directly related to one's job. She further elaborates that job-embedded learning should be ongoing and collaborative to have the most benefit. She finds her interpretation of learning experiences is also influenced by the culture and context of her work environment.

The learning logs submitted by Emily reveal her preference for independent study; however, she notes several instances of collaborative job-embedded learning. For instance, she includes the following as sources of learning in her logs: content, grade-level, and faculty meetings; digital learning modules and videos; and informal peer collaboration. One of her learning log entries details the ease of use, value, and flexibility digital learning modules have and the influence they've had on her teaching practice. The digital learning modules provide her with an opportunity to examine new teaching curriculum and pedagogy as well as collaborate with other teachers via blogs and wikis. Emily's experiences illustrate how learning experiences and sensemaking can occur beyond the physical walls of one's school.

CROSS-CASE ANALYSIS

Cross-case analysis considers the findings from each participant's case to identify patterns in the overall data. Five themes emerged through collective data analysis and represent the processes or influences that guided each teacher's co-construction of new knowledge and skills. Although these themes typically occurred concurrently, each theme is presented as a disaggregated section for depth and clarity. The five themes include identity, motivation, reflection, collaboration, and application.

Theme 1: Identity

Teachers make sense of and give meaning to their job-embedded learning experiences using their worldview, beliefs, and understandings to negotiate and construct new knowledge and skills. Teachers express how initial teacher preparation helped to shape their teaching identity and, subsequently, their interpretation of learning experiences.

For instance, Amanda's experience in a Cooperative Urban Teacher Education program, in which she engages in community service and outreach, offers her a unique perspective of the community and students she teaches. She attributes this experience to her developing a do-whatever-it-takes attitude for ensuring the success of her students. Her desire to learn and do more makes her self-motivated and innovative, thus encouraging her to engage in job-embedded learning whenever a formal or informal opportunity arises.

Teachers also note how their beginning years of teaching influence their teaching identity and interpretation of learning experiences. For example, Leslie's experiences teaching at a low-income, rural elementary school and an urban middle school during her first five years of teaching prompt her to reflect on and refine her teaching practices to meet her students' needs. She describes how reflecting on her strengths and weaknesses contributes to her overall identity and her desire to engage in professional learning for personal betterment.

In summary, a teacher's identity facilitates self-awareness and influences the interpretations and actions of that teacher's learning experiences. Initial preparation programs and the experiences teachers have during their first few years of teaching provide the foundation of their teaching identity and ultimately determine how and why they engage in professional learning.

Theme 2: Motivation

Teachers make sense of and give meaning to their job-embedded learning experiences when motivated intrinsically and extrinsically. Specifically, self-improvement, a passion for teaching, annual evaluations, and the need to strengthen their teaching practices motivate teachers to engage in professional learning. For instance, Amanda states how she reads current literature and books on pedagogy to improve her teaching, while Emily searches for new technology, interactive links, and apps to use with her students. Teachers are motivated to learn when their personal interests and motivations align with the learning experience. Sensemaking of the learning experience is also enhanced since the teachers find relevance in the work.

Consequently, lack of motivation can hinder learning when teachers are obligated to participate in learning experiences that are not relevant to their work, lack context, or provide little or no support or application in practice. For example, Sarah shares a learning experience in which she had to learn how to implement a new literacy approach in the classroom. As a science and social studies teacher, she describes the experience as negative since she could not find relevance in the topic.

Likewise, Leslie elaborates on a similar experience regarding technology in which no follow-up or feedback was provided to ensure successful implementation in practice; thus, she never revisited it. Sarah and Leslie's experiences demonstrate how sensemaking of job-embedded learning can be limited if the content or delivery isn't right. Both teachers believe that they will be more motivated to participate in a learning experience if the facilitator considers their learning preferences, interests, and skills when planning and delivering the content.

Overall, teacher motivation considers the relevancy and applicability of a new learning experience and explains why teachers engage in job-embedded learning. Motivation can have a positive or negative impact on job-embedded learning experiences; thus, it's essential to consider both content and structure.

Theme 3: Reflection

Teachers make sense of and give meaning to their job-embedded learning by reflecting on prior beliefs, understandings, and experiences. Reflection during and following a learning experience helps teachers acquire new knowledge and skills. To illustrate, Leslie reflects on what she learned by mentoring a student teacher several years ago. She finds meaning and value in working with pre-service teachers because it challenges her to take risks and keep current with the latest instructional strategies. Her experiences highlight how central reflection is to the sensemaking of what teachers do and learn as they engage in the work of being a teacher.

Similarly, Amanda reflects on how in her current classroom she applied her training in the Socratic method from years earlier. She noticed that her gifted students needed a challenge, so she dug deep into her memory toolbox to uncover old strategies. Her ability to recall and apply past knowledge and skills in a new context highlight the advantages job-embedded learning can have on teaching practice.

Reflection fosters the negotiation and melding of new and old learning experiences by encouraging the teacher to think about prior beliefs, understandings, and experiences within a new context. Reflection is central to teacher sensemaking since it strongly influences how the teacher approaches and applies new knowledge and skills.

Theme 4: Collaboration

Teachers make sense of and give meaning to their job-embedded learning experiences as they collaborate and interact with colleagues. For instance, in a more formal sense, Sarah and Emily both share how collaboration during weekly content team meetings helps them combat feelings of isolation by supporting and encouraging them to take risks and try new instructional strategies. They use the content team meetings to share experiences, ask questions, and seek support or ideas on how to refine their current teaching practice or implement new knowledge and skills in their classroom.

Collaboration also takes a more informal form for many of the teachers as they compare experiences and check in with each other during class changes, lunch, and in the teacher work room. For example, Leslie comments on how she came to implement choice boards and close reading in her social studies lessons by talking with colleagues and visiting their classrooms. How she makes sense of and gives meaning to what she hears and what she observes are enhanced by her willingness to learn from her colleagues.

Overall, teacher collaboration provides support for new learning experiences while challenging teachers to think about how their interactions and conversation influence their teaching practices. Collaboration can either positively or negatively influence learning experiences in both formal and informal settings. Thus, collaboration is essential to the teacher's sensemaking of learning experiences.

Theme 5: Application

Teachers make sense of and give meaning to job-embedded learning experiences that are relevant and applicable to their job. For example, Sarah summarizes the connection between applicability and sensemaking by conveying the benefit of content team meetings in providing her with a safe space where she can share ideas and seek help. She finds the structure of the meetings as one in which problems can be discussed and solutions generated by the group. The learning experience gives her confidence, encouragement, and support.

Amanda describes how conversations in a book study group encourage her to try new pedagogical ideas in her classroom as well as share her learning with her colleagues. She finds value and applicability in the book studies because she is interested in the content of the book and invested in trying out the ideas in her classroom. How Amanda makes sense of and gives meaning to her experiences in the classroom is guided by her understanding of the book's content, her success and failures in implementing the ideas in her classroom, and the perspectives of her peers sharing the learning experience.

In summary, the application or transferability of the learning experience encourages teachers to establish a purpose for learning something new and to identify a course of action for acquiring and applying this knowledge and these skills in practice. Learning experiences that attend to relevance, coherence, and duration have a greater chance of successful transferability and give teachers the confidence and support they need to seek out and try new resources in their classroom.

DISCUSSION OF FINDINGS

A lot of research examines the key features of effective professional development and the characteristics of job-embedded learning; however, the purpose of this study was to discover teachers' sensemaking of learning experiences that occur during the school day as they engage in the work of being a teacher. Based on this study, five conclusions are offered.

Teachers make sense of and give meaning to new learning experiences using their worldview, beliefs, and understandings to negotiate and co-construct new knowledge and skills. Initial teacher preparation and the first few years of teaching significantly influence teachers' identities, including their philosophies of teaching and learning. Furthermore, teachers' identities are responsible for their perceptions of students, the roles and functions of school, and the expectation and impact of professional learning on teaching practice.

Related studies present similar findings regarding teacher identity. Teachers need an understanding of their identity—their worldview, beliefs, and understanding of prior experiences—to negotiate and construct new knowledge and skills via practice (Coburn, 2005; Mitchell, 2014). Further, teachers' identities are so essential to sensemaking and interpretation of learning experiences that misunderstanding or misinterpretation may occur if teachers' identities do not align with that of others (Schmidt & Datnow, 2005).

Teachers make sense of and give meaning to new learning experiences when motivated, both intrinsically and extrinsically, to engage in relevant and coherent job-embedded learning. Teachers' motivation to learn and apply new knowledge and skills coincides with their desire to improve their teaching practice, avoid the social stigma of failure, or meet a mandated obligation or requirement. Interestingly, teachers' motivation to engage in job-embedded learning relies on their interest in the content to make sense of the learning experience, regardless of whether the content is relevant or ongoing or includes opportunities for collaboration and application.

Current research does not specifically link motivation and sensemaking; however, many studies note that job-embedded learning is most effective when it adheres to adult learning principles (Darling-Hammond & McLaughlin, 2011; Zepeda, 2017). Adults are self-directed learners who are motivated to participate in learning experiences that provide content focused on tasks that relate to their daily lives. Thus, teachers' motivations and identities are essential to understanding the sensemaking of job-embedded learning experiences.

Teachers make sense of and give meaning to new learning experiences by reflecting on prior beliefs, understandings, and experiences to meld new and old teaching practices. Teachers reflect when determining how to implement a new teaching strategy, recalling ways to teach a concept or improve their teaching of it, and thinking of how to solve a problem in practice. The process of reflection encourages teachers to consider and share their past and current teaching practices as well as devise plans for revising and improving it.

Reflection is a key feature of job-embedded learning and improves teachers' ability to transfer and apply new knowledge and skills to practice (Coggshall et al., 2012; Zepeda, 2015). Further, reflection is critical to teachers' sensemaking of learning experiences as it requires them to evaluate their viewpoints and (re)align them with new information (Colestock & Sherin, 2009; Mitchell, 2014).

Teachers make sense of and give meaning to new learning experiences as they collaborate with colleagues to refine and challenge their teaching practices. Teachers informally and formally engage in dialogue with colleagues via hallway check-ins, impromptu classroom visits, collaborative meetings, and book studies. Regardless of format, teacher collaboration not only influences teachers' sensemaking of learning experiences but also improves their overall understanding. Collaboration also helps teachers refine their teaching practices by providing them with the ongoing support needed for successful implementation.

In the literature, collaboration is a significant factor in determining the sensemaking of a learning experience since it exposes teachers to different perspectives and experiences that might challenge their current beliefs, understanding, or teaching practices (Coburn, 2005; Mitchell, 2014). Additionally, job-embedded learning experiences that include collaborative elements result in improved classroom practices, a better understanding of content and pedagogy, more opportunities for feedback and support, and increased teacher empowerment (Mawhinney, 2010).

Teachers make sense of and give meaning to new learning experiences when they engage in job-embedded learning that is applicable to their work as a teacher. Teachers prefer learning experiences that directly relate to their interests, professional goals, and classroom context. Teachers do not favor learning experiences if they are not given opportunities to apply, practice, and receive feedback on their new knowledge and skills.

Current research asserts that providing ongoing support and feedback to teachers enhances their sensemaking of learning experiences and gives them confidence to take risks (Coburn & Woulfin, 2012; Mitchell, 2014). Moreover, teachers who engage in relevant, coherent, and embedded learning experiences are more likely to implement new knowledge and skills since there is a strong connection between theory and practice (Mizell, 2010).

IMPLICATIONS FOR SCHOOL LEADERS

There are numerous implications here for how the learning experiences of teachers can be facilitated and supported by school leaders. First, administrators may find value in the findings regarding how teachers construct an understanding of their job-embedded learning experiences since the role of administrators has shifted to that of instructional leader (Zepeda, 2017). Administrators need to consider teacher identity and motivation when designing and implementing job-embedded learning experiences.

Furthermore, administrators should think about how their own identity and motivations influence the delivery and implementation of job-embedded learning experiences—as several teachers in the study commented when discussing presenter influence. Overall, attending to teacher identity and motivation may increase the likelihood that a given teacher will find a learning experience meaningful and valuable, even if that experience challenges the teacher to reconsider his or her prior notions.

Administrators might consider the use of personality, learning style, or motivational surveys to learn more about the worldview, beliefs, understandings, and interests of their faculty prior to developing and implementing professional development. Learning more about the background and experiences that have shaped a teacher can lead to more personalized, and differentiated, learning experiences. The current study found that teachers desired job-embedded learning experiences that reflect their professional wants and needs while adhering to the key features of effective professional development.

The findings also highlight the importance of reflection, collaboration, and application to the sensemaking process. Administrators should designate time for oral and written reflection and feedback, provide ongoing and purposeful opportunities for collaboration in a variety of formats, and strive to design learning experiences focused on applying new knowledge and skills in practice rather than isolation.

The findings of reflection, collaboration, and application support the key features of effective professional development: content focus, active learning, coherence, duration, and collective participation. They serve as reminders of how the features of job-embedded learning, grounded in practice and daily reflection, promote collegiality, facilitate application and adaptation, and help teachers construct new knowledge and skills.

SUMMARY

This study examined how four middle school teachers constructed understandings of their job-embedded learning experiences that occurred while engaged in the work of being a teacher. Findings reveal five influences that affect teachers' sensemaking and give meaning to their experiences: identity, motivation, reflection, collaboration, and application. While each influence affects teacher sensemaking independently, each influence often intertwines with and compliments the other.

Teacher identity is found to initiate the sensemaking process as teachers examine their worldview, beliefs, and understanding to negotiate and co-construct new knowledge and skills. Teacher motivation proves to be a significant finding as it often determines what professional learning teachers engage in and how meaningful they find the experience. Teacher reflection focuses on melding old and new learning experiences by using a teacher's identity and motivation as a starting point.

Collaboration provides support for learning experiences and challenges teachers to explore how their interactions and conversations influence teaching practice. Finally, application encourages teachers to identify a purpose for learning and develop a plan for acquiring and implementing new knowledge and skills.

Overall, the findings of this study highlight the impact job-embedded learning can have on teaching practice. Job-embedded learning is a viable way to support professional learning that is ongoing, relevant, and embedded within the context of a teacher's workday. As such, its situated nature encourages teachers continuously to update and refine their teaching knowledge and skills with a focus on student achievement.

Discussion Questions

1. Identify the job-embedded learning experiences that occur at your school. How do these learning experiences improve the knowledge, skills, and teaching practices of faculty?
2. What can school leaders do to ensure that job-embedded learning considers teachers' identity and motivation while providing ample opportunities for reflection, collaboration, and application?
3. What role should teachers, teacher leaders, and administrators assume to ensure the successful implementation of job-embedded learning?

SUGGESTED READINGS

Coggshall, J. G., Rasmussen, C., Colton, A., Milton, J., & Jacques, C. (2012). *Generating teaching effectiveness: The role of job-embedded professional learning in teacher evaluation.* Washington, DC: National Comprehensive Center for Teacher Quality. Retrieved from http://www.tqsource.org/publications/GeneratingTeachingEffectiveness.pdf

Gulamhussein, A. (2013). Teaching the teachers: Effective professional development in an era of high stakes accountability. Alexandria, VA: National School Board Association Center for Public Education. Retrieved from http://www.centerforpubliceducation.org/teachingtheteachers

Guskey, T. R. (2014). Planning professional learning. *Educational Leadership, 71*(8), 10–16. Retrieved from http://www.ascd.org/publications/educational-leadership/may14/vol71/num08/Planning-Professional-Learning.aspx

REFERENCES

Choo, C. W. (2006). *The knowing organization: How organizations use information to construct meaning, create knowledge, and make decisions* (2nd ed.). New York, NY: Oxford University Press.

Coburn, C. E. (2005). Shaping teacher sensemaking: School leaders and the enactment of reading policy. *Educational Policy, 19*(3), 476–509. doi:10.1177/0895904805276143

Coburn, C. E., & Woulfin, S. L. (2012). Reading coaches and the relationship between policy and practice. *Reading Research Quarterly, 47*(1), 5–30. doi:10.1002/RRQ.008

Coggshall, J. G., Rasmussen, C., Colton, A., Milton, J., & Jacques, C. (2012). *Generating teaching effectiveness: The role of job-embedded professional learning in teacher evaluation.* Washington, DC: National Comprehensive Center for Teacher Quality. Retrieved from http://www.tqsource.org/publications/GeneratingTeachingEffectiveness.pdf

Colestock, A., & Sherin, M. G. (2009). Teachers' sense-making strategies while watching video of mathematics instruction. *Journal of Technology and Teacher Education, 17*(1), 7–29. Retrieved from http://www.editlib.org/p/26234

Corbin, J. M., & Strauss, A. L. (2008). *Basics of qualitative research: Techniques and procedures for developing grounded theory* (3rd ed.). Los Angeles, CA: Sage Publications.

Creswell, J. W. (2007). *Qualitative inquiry & research design: Choosing among five approaches* (2nd ed.). Thousand Oaks, CA: Sage Publications.

Darling-Hammond, L., & McLaughlin, M. W. (2011). Policies that support professional development in an era of reform. *Phi Delta Kappan, 92*(6), 81–92. (Reprinted from *Phi Delta Kappan, 76*[8], 597–604). doi:10.1177/003172171109200622

Darling-Hammond, L., Wei, R. C., Andree, A., Richardson, N., & Orphanos, S. (2009). *Professional learning in the learning profession: A status report on teacher development in the United States and abroad.* Dallas, TX: National Staff Development Council. Retrieved from http://www.srnleads.org/resources/publications/pdf/nsdc_profdev_tech_report.pdf

Ginsberg, M. B., & Wlodkowski, R. J. (2010). Access and participation. In C. E. Kasworm, A. D. Rose, & J. M. Ross-Gordon (Eds.), *Handbook of adult and continuing education* (pp. 25–34). Thousand Oaks, CA: Sage Publications.

Glaser, B. G., & Strauss, A. L. (1967). *The discovery of grounded theory: Strategies for qualitative research.* Piscataway, NJ: AldineTransaction.

Glickman, C. D., Gordon, S. P., & Ross-Gordon, J. M. (2009). *Supervision of instruction: A developmental approach* (7th ed.). Boston, MA: Allyn and Bacon.

Gulamhussein, A. (2013). Teaching the teachers: Effective professional development in an era of high stakes accountability. Alexandria, VA: National School Board Association Center for Public Education. Retrieved from http://www.centerforpubliceducation.org/teachingtheteachers

Guskey, T. R. (2014). Planning professional learning. *Educational Leadership, 71*(8), 10–16. Retrieved from http://www.ascd.org/publications/educational-leadership/may14/vol71/num08/Planning-Professional-Learning.aspx

Guskey, T. R., & Yoon, K. S. (2009). What works in professional development? *Phi Delta Kappan, 90*(7), 495–500. doi:10.1177/003172170909000709

Hunzicker, J. (2011). Effective professional development for teachers: A checklist. *Professional Development in Education, 37*(2), 177–179. doi:10.1080/19415257.2010.523955

Jackson, A., & Davis, G. A. (2000). *Turning points 2000: Educating adolescents in the 21st Century.* New York, NY: Teachers College Press.

Mawhinney, L. (2010). Let's lunch and learn: Professional knowledge sharing in teachers' lounges and other congregational spaces. *Teaching and teacher education: An international journal of research and studies, 26*(4), 972–978. doi: 10.1016/j.tate.2009.10.039

Mitchell, T. D. (2014). How service-learning enacts social justice sensemaking. *Journal of Critical Thought and Praxis, 2*(2), 4. Retrieved from http://lib.dr.iastate.edu/jctp/vol2/iss2/6/

Mizell, H. (2010). *Why professional development matters.* Oxford, OH: Learning Forward. Retrieved from http://learningforward.org/docs/pdf/why_pd_matters_web.pdf?sfvrsn=0

National Institute for Excellence in Teaching. (2012). *Beyond "job-embedded": Ensuring that good professional development gets results.* Santa Monica, CA: National Institute for Excellence in Teaching. Retrieved from http://www.niet.org/assets/PDFs/beyond_job_embedded_professional_development.pdf

National Middle School Association. (2010). *This we believe: Keys to educating young adolescents.* Westerville, OH: National Middle School Association.

Pate, P. E., & Thompson, K. F. (2003). Effective professional development: What is it? In P. G. Andrews & V. A. Anfara (Eds.), *Leaders for a movement: Professional preparation and development of middle level teachers and administrators* (pp. 123–143). Greenwich, CT: Information Age Publishing.

Schmidt, M., & Datnow, A. (2005). Teachers' sense-making about comprehensive school reform: The influence of emotions. *Teaching and Teacher Education, 21*(8), 949–965. doi: 10.1016/j.tate.2005.06.006

Wei, R. C., Darling-Hammond, L., & Adamson, F. (2010). *Professional development in the United States: Trends and challenges.* Dallas, TX: National Staff Development Council. Retrieved from https://edpolicy.stanford.edu/publications/pubs/89

Weick, K. E. (2012). Organized sensemaking: A commentary on processes of interpretive work. *Human Relations, 65*(1), 141–154. doi:10.1177/0018726711424235

Wood, F. H., & McQuarrie, F. O. Jr. (1999). On-the-job learning. *Journal of Staff Development, 20*(3), 10–13. Retrieved from https://learningforward.org/publications/jsd

Yin, R. K. (2009). *Case study research: Design and methods* (4th ed.). Los Angeles, CA: Sage Publications.

Zepeda, S. J. (2015). *Job-embedded professional development: Support, collaboration, and learning in schools.* New York, NY: Routledge.

Zepeda, S. J. (2017). *Instructional supervision: Applying tools and concepts* (4th ed.). New York, NY: Routledge.

Chapter 3

Creating Coherence Between Teacher Evaluation and Ongoing Teacher Learning by Engaging in Collegial Goal Groups

Jen Cole

SCENARIO

After school, the professional learning room is a buzz of activity with Heather, Marcus, Tonya, and Lisa sitting together at one of the tables. They are one of six groups of teachers that have been working collaboratively on a goal common to each group to improve their teaching practice.

Heather is the group's facilitator for this meeting: "Today we will each share a strategy we have tried and how it went in the classroom. Lisa, would you get us started?" Lisa remembers what setting goals was like before goal groups: "Filling out that goal form at the beginning of the year didn't mean anything. It was filed in some notebook in the office. I couldn't even remember what my goal was by the end of the year.

This year, she wanted students to be more involved in their learning so they would remember more of the lesson and know how to apply that knowledge. She thought, "I have learned so much by working in my group. It's only December and already I have so many more strategies than I did."

KEY IDEAS IN THIS CHAPTER

- Teachers value setting their own professional learning goals.
- Synergy between individual and collaborative work propels learning forward at the individual and group level.
- Goal group professional learning supports coherence between evaluation, goal setting, and professional learning.

ABSTRACT

This qualitative study sought to understand how teachers perceive the pursuit of individual professional goals in a collegial group setting as a form of job-embedded professional learning. Five themes revealed teachers' perceptions of their participation in goal group professional learning. (1) Teachers valued the collaborative process of goal groups even while they encountered barriers. (2) Supportive, professional teacher relationships and networks created positive shifts in school culture. (3) The intersection between individual and collaborative work propelled learning forward at the individual and group level. (4) Goal group professional learning supported coherence between evaluation, goal setting, and professional learning. (5) Teachers made lasting changes in their teaching practice and beliefs about teaching.

INTRODUCTION

This study examined goal groups. Goal groups are a professional learning sequence based on a traditional school year. The objective of goal groups is to move professional learning beyond merely delivering or covering content. Teachers develop annual goals at the beginning of a school year as part of the teacher evaluation system. The goals determine teacher placement in topic-based learning groups called "goal groups."

The purpose of this study was to understand how teachers perceived the pursuit of individual professional goals in a collegial setting as a means of job-embedded professional learning. Teachers' perspectives on their participation in goal groups were examined. Building on past research regarding collaborative job-embedded professional learning and its impact on individual learning, this study provided an opportunity to look at a possible bridge between individual teachers' experiences in collaborative settings that support growth embedded as a formative process of a teacher evaluation system.

OVERVIEW OF THE LITERATURE

The positive impact of teacher quality on student achievement is established in the literature (Darling-Hammond, 2010; Harris & Sass, 2011). The key to building and maintaining teacher quality is effective and ongoing professional learning (Glickman, Gordon, & Ross-Gordon, 2012; Guskey, 2011). To promote teacher quality, professional development practices should support the sustained growth of individual teachers (Bayar, 2014; Zepeda, 2012).

Teacher learning is a process by which teachers identify, test, employ, and understand new ideas about teaching (Darling-Hammond, 2010; Zepeda, 2012). For teachers to learn, they need to see and experience a connection between acquiring new knowledge and implementing it. Consequently, effective professional development must be based on adult learning theories that support connections between the need for learning, the actual learning, and experiences in an authentic environment. The literature, when examined across disciplines, implies an inherent link between goal setting, job-embedded professional learning, cooperative learning, and coherence.

Goal Setting

One of adult learning's key principles is that adults are able to determine their own needs for learning (Brookfield, 2013). Goal setting is a form of adult, self-directed learning required in many teacher evaluation systems (Grant, 2012; Zepeda, 2017). Goal-setting theory refers to the effects of setting goals on subsequent performance (Locke & Latham, 2013).

Self-concordance is defined as the degree to which goal alignment is connected with an individual's interests, motivations, and needs. It is a crucial element necessary for goal attainment. Self-concordance emphasizes the extent to which the individual perceives goals as being determined by internal or external factors. The greater the self-concordance, the more likely goal attainment will be achieved (Grant, 2012).

The act of setting learning goals is about learners becoming active participants in the learning process. Parker, Jimmieson, and Amiot (2009) found that autonomy with goal setting in the workplace improves self-efficacy. This in turn improves the likelihood of goal attainment.

Job-Embedded Professional Development

Job-embedded professional development is defined as teacher learning grounded in teachers' day-to-day teaching experience (Whitfield & Wood, 2010). Croft, Coggshall, Dolan, and Powers (2010) explained that job-embedded professional development is "largely a product of formal and informal social interactions among teachers, situated in the context of their school and the classrooms in which they teach and is distributed across the entire staff" (p. 5).

Job-embedded professional development increases student achievement and empowers teachers to collaborate and reflect on the improvement of instructional practices (Darling-Hammond & McLaughlin, 2011; Hirsh, 2009;

Hord, 2009; Zepeda, 2012). Job-embedded professional learning intellectually engages teachers in cycles of action and reflection. Through this work, teachers build relationships that support and encourage continuous improvement in teaching and learning (Sparks, 2013).

Cooperative Learning

Cooperative learning became a commonly used way to organize learning experiences in the 1980s, and it continues to be a valuable method for learning in multiple situations (Johnson, Johnson, & Smith, 2007). Slavin (2014) defined cooperative learning as a teaching method in which learners work together in small groups to help one another learn. Research on effective professional development emphasizes the importance of collaborative and collegial learning environments that help develop communities of practice able to promote school-wide change (Darling-Hammond, Wei, Andree, Richardson, & Orphanos, 2009).

Teachers need ample collaborative opportunities to figure out and solve problems related to classroom issues. This time allows teachers to work together to discover connections between instruction and student outcomes (Gallimore, Ermeling, Saunders, & Goldenberg, 2009). Not only are teachers solving their own classroom concerns, but they were also creating and sharing lasting change in instructional practices.

Coherence

Desimone (2011) outlines three dimensions of coherence that are critical for effective teacher professional development. (1) New learning should build on what teachers already know. (2) Professional development should align "with national, state, and local standards; assessment; curriculum; and other reforms" (p. 65). And (3) professional development should "support sustained professional communication among teachers who are working to reform their teaching in similar ways" (p. 65).

CONTEXT OF THE STUDY

This study takes place in a school district that serves about 13,500 students. There are approximately 450 students at this elementary school, which includes kindergarten through fifth grade. About 49% of the students are African American, 26% Hispanic, and 18% Caucasian, while the remaining students are multiracial. Eighty-five percent of the students are eligible for free or reduced lunches.

Table 3.1 Goal Group Process

Teachers set goals and were placed in teacher learning groups based on common goals.
Teachers worked within these groups to establish learning needs and objectives.
An instructional coach worked with the teachers to find learning materials and other opportunities to further learning.
Teachers worked face-to-face and in e-learning communities with an instructional coach and teacher leaders.
Teachers experimented with new practices based on learning.
Teachers shared experiences and learning in formal goal group meetings.
Teachers observed other teachers within the groups to further learning around goals.
Teachers worked in teams to consider artifacts in preparation for annual evaluations.
Teachers met with the principal for a final evaluation.
Teachers shared goal group learning with other teachers outside their goal groups

There are 33 teachers at the school. Of these 33 teachers, 24 hold advanced degrees. The teachers average 12 years of experience. In the school, 30 teachers participated in goal group professional learning. These 30 teachers were divided into six groups based on their selected goals. The teachers at the school developed annual goals at the beginning of the year as part of the teacher evaluation system within the school district. The goals determined teacher placement in topic-based learning groups called "goal groups." Teachers engaged in goal-based, collaborative, professional learning throughout the academic year. Table 3.1 outlines the yearlong, goal group sequence.

RESEARCH METHODS

An interpretive case study design was used to describe in detail the experiences of teachers working in goal groups. A case study approach is particularly useful in examining loosely coupled systems (Hamilton & Whittier, 2013) as in the present study that examined professional learning coupled with a teacher evaluation system often considered detrimental to growth and development (Zepeda, 2017). In this study, teachers participated in goal groups associated with their individual goals, and each group maintained an identity or separateness from the other groups; however, there was sharing within and between the groups.

The four types of data collection for this study included

- participant interviews: five teachers representing different goal groups and grade levels participated in two interviews that lasted between 45 and 60 minutes each. One of the interviews occurred at the beginning of the year as goal groups were beginning and the other at the end of the year. In the interviews, teachers were asked about teacher group goals, professional development, teacher learning, and teacher networks.
- focus groups: five teachers different from those already interviewed participated in an hour-long focus group during the middle of the school year. The focus group was a semistructured interview in which all five participants answered open-ended questions in a conversational manner, followed by a certain set of questions related to group goals, professional development, teacher learning, and teacher networks.
- participant observations: the interviewed teachers were also observed in goal group meetings. Participant observations took place during regularly scheduled goal group meetings. Three hours of participant observations were recorded from four different goal group meetings. The meetings were recorded using video and audio for repeated review.
- document review: official documents related to goal groups provided additional data. During the process of working on goals, teachers used a shared electronic filing system to maintain documentation of their learning and progress toward meeting their goals. Participants also kept a record of goals set, work toward the goals, and any assistance they requested. These documents were already part of the goal group process and had the potential to reveal teacher thinking about goals and if shifts were made in teacher practices related to teachers' goals.

Thematic analysis was used to code and then to analyze sections of text according to whether they appeared to contribute to emerging themes (Schwandt, 2007). The process began with a close reading of the texts from interviews, and the data were then organized into categories that were then further synthesized and distilled to identify themes across the data.

FINDINGS

Five themes emerged revealing teachers' perceptions of their participation in goal group professional learning. The themes are presented here with analysis.

Theme 1: Teachers valued the collaborative process of goal groups even when they encountered barriers related to time, increased difficulty in planning, and frustration with group members.

Teachers identified several barriers to working in goal groups. Finding time to work on goals, planning and implementing new learning, and reflecting on the experiences between goal group meetings while maintaining all other teaching responsibilities was challenging to teachers. Despite these barriers, teachers found value in goal group professional learning. Nina said, "I guess maybe all of us are saying the learning and planning is time-consuming and hard, but I think the fruit that comes from it, it's very worthwhile."

Teachers expressed a strong sense of accountability from working in goal groups. Alex said, "Even if it's just reduced to accountability, I think that's big." The consistency of meetings and the pressure of working with peers contributes to feelings of accountability and a subsequent sense of accomplishment.

Teachers valued how their participation in goal groups had an impact on classroom instruction and student learning. Halle noted, "I believe that any time spent sharing with colleagues is progress toward professional growth." Teachers identified time as a barrier but recognized the value of investing time as a benefit to themselves and students. Teachers recognized the impact of participating in goal group professional learning on their classroom instruction.

Theme 2: The continued development of teacher relationships and networks connected to professional practice created positive shifts in school culture.

Taking steps to develop teacher relationships and networks while building collective capacity for instruction created positive shifts in school culture. Highly functioning professional learning groups created a cycle of influence among the key players within a school. Data suggested that as the practices of individual teachers improved, so too did the practices of the other members of the goal groups.

When goal group professional learning began, not all of the teachers were excited about the work. As example, Chloe said that in the beginning, "I was like 'Oh, man, I don't want to do this. Ugh!'" During the year, Chloe's opinion of goal group professional learning changed to "It's beneficial to everyone that's involved." Even though Chloe did not want to participate in the beginning, the benefit she found in the collaborative process changed her opinion. Data across participants echoed Chloe's sentiments.

Teachers identified the elements of collaboration they valued:

- the intrinsic motivation that comes from accountability to a group;
- the increased focus and learning that comes from discussions about pedagogy; and

- the nonjudgmental support of working with peers to solve problems.

When professionals work together to improve practice, both the individual and group improve. Halle explained, "We are all doing one thing together," and Lisa suggested, "We're sharing what we've figured out and whether it worked out or not."

Another important piece of a positive school-culture cycle is the support of the administrative team. All participants acknowledged the need to feel supported in risk taking. Learning and implementing new pedagogy required teachers to step out of their comfort zone and live with some anxiety. It takes time to gain a sense of mastery. Alex said, "So I feel like there is support for people who are learning, and I feel like there are realistic expectations for risk taking."

Theme 3: The intersection between individual and collaborative work propelled learning forward at the individual and group level.

Teachers engaged in individual and collaborative learning activities while participating in goal groups. Individual learning is defined in this discussion as the work teachers do outside of working with goal group members on goals. The collaborative processes of goal groups were the activities that happened when teachers worked together either in the formal setting of goal group meetings or in the informal work that teachers did together outside meetings.

The individual and collaborative experiences of teachers run in cycles of individual and collaborative work, which creates synergy. Figure 3.1 illustrates the relationship between individual and collaborative experiences in goal groups and the synergy that is created. The synergic outcomes of goal groups offered teachers peer support to take risks, built capacity for learning, accelerated the spread of instructional knowledge, and developed teacher networks beyond goal groups.

Changing classroom practices initially caused some teachers to enter a state of disequilibrium because they did not have the competency and confidence to implement change on their own. The increased sense of risk inherent in new learning produced varying levels of anxiety in teachers. The peer support offered through collaborative work allowed teachers to develop new ways of addressing problems in their classrooms and a sense of safety in struggling through the implementation. Teachers expressed feelings of connection and comfort in knowing that other teachers were struggling with similar questions.

The cross-grade structure of goal group professional learning accelerated the spread of instructional knowledge. Teachers participated in a cycle of working with their goal group on their goal and returning to their grade-level teams. As teachers learned new ideas and strategies, they talked to their

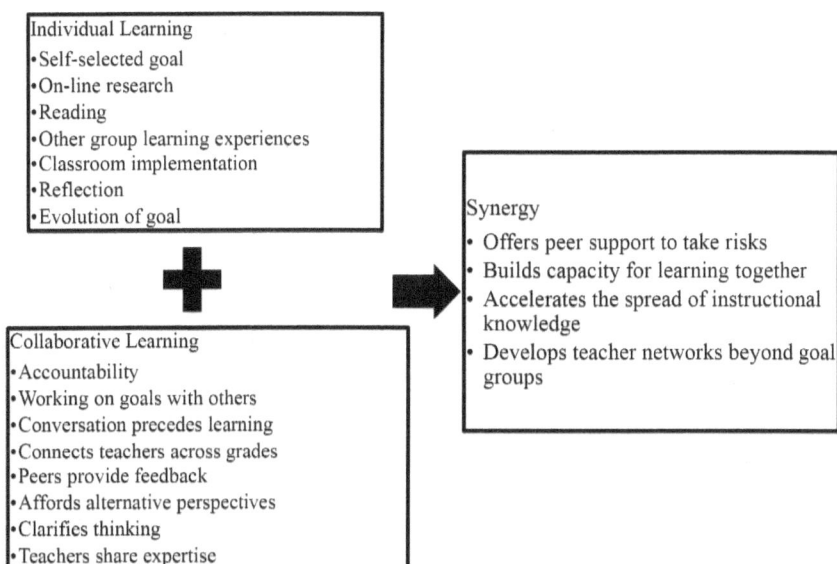

Figure 3.1   Individual + Collaborative = Synergy

grade-level teams and implemented the learning into lesson plans for the grade level. Within grade-level teams, teachers learned from the members of their grade-level team then returned to share with their goal group.

The intersection between individual and collaborative work propelled learning forward at the individual and group level. Teachers believed they had the support of their group, learned and implemented new ways of teaching and connecting with students, shared the learning across the school, and developed more and more teacher support along the way.

Theme 4: Goal group professional learning supported coherence between evaluation, goal setting, and professional learning.

Goal group professional learning is a path that connects a goal to professional learning and to evaluation. Coherence is defined by how well expectations of teachers, their professional learning activities, and teachers' own goals for themselves and their students align. The teacher evaluation system in place at this school was predicated on a growth model. In this model, the teacher is at the center of an evaluation positioned as an overall effort to improve instructional practices. At the beginning of the year, the teacher met with the administrator. The teacher reflected on past performance and selected an area in which they would like to grow or strengthen their teaching practices.

Teachers drew from the set of standards used in the teacher evaluation system to determine goals that were related to their classroom practices.

Halle explained, "The district wants us to be able to do this, this, and this. So, I would look and see, okay, so what do I feel like I need to work on to meet what the district want me to do?" The data illustrated that teachers decided on goals based on feedback from their administrator and reflection on their own practice.

The most important aspect to teachers making a decision about goals is that they have the final say in setting goals. Madge said, "I do think we are stronger in our commitment to our goals if we pick them. Giving us the choice makes it more positive and more motivating." Similarly, Alex stated, "[My goal group] was one of the few ways I had to connect with my peers, professionally, over a topic we had chosen, that was our own choice, so we bought into that."

Teachers described goal groups as a place to introduce real problems they had in the classroom. Emily said, "I felt like I could come talk about 'I don't know how to make this work. I don't know how to reach these kids. I don't know what do to.' My group would help me figure it out." Emily's description of her experience in goal groups directly connected her goals for learning with her professional development activities. This level of coherence had an impact on her teaching.

At the end of the year, teachers meet again with the administrator for a final evaluation. While teachers felt prepared to meet with the administrator at the end of the year, what was more important is how they felt about their own learning facilitated through goal group professional learning. When asked about learning in goal groups at the end of the year, Alex said,

> I thought, "Good job!" I think that was part of the point of it, was to make you intentionally think through the things you've done, what you've tried, how much effort you've put into it, and how far you've come with it. It was very affirming to me. I felt like the process made me accountable and it helped me realize, instead of what I hadn't done, it helped me realize what I had done.

The process of goal groups tied together the goal, professional learning, and teacher change as shared in the final evaluation at the end of the year.

Theme 5: Teachers not only made lasting changes in their teaching practice, but they also made shifts in their beliefs about teaching.

Teachers implemented learning from goal groups in their teaching, which teachers then reported as having an impact on students. Teachers not only made lasting changes in their teaching practice, they also made changes in their beliefs about teaching. Alex explained, "I definitely think that working on the goal that I worked on impacted the way that I taught and the amount of learning that happened."

Teachers made changes that they believed had a positive impact on student learning. Teachers who had participated in goal groups in previous years additionally provided examples of how the previous years' goal group work continued to have an influence on their teaching. Teachers shared lasting changes made to their practice. Beth gave an example from her work of the previous year in the classroom community goal group: "Last year, I implemented things like a closing circle and student reflections. Now, those things are just part of our routine." Teachers made long-term changes to what they were doing in their classrooms.

DISCUSSION OF FINDINGS

The results of this study suggest that goal group professional learning, if properly structured and supported by administrators, can contribute to individual and collaborative teacher learning. Additionally, the results indicate that teachers value collaboration and that collaboration connected to professional practice can create positive shifts in a school culture. Finally, a very strong correlation emerged between changes in instructional practice and reported increases in student learning. The findings have implications for policy, practice, and future research that are addressed in the following sections.

Collaboration Is Essential to Goal Groups

Collaboration is a critical element of goal group professional learning. Teachers valued collaboration, identifying benefits that included increased accountability and more sustained conversations about teaching. The participants also identified developing relationships with teachers beyond their grade-level teams and the impact the work had on their teaching.

Individual and group accountability was key to each group's overall success and ultimately to the success of each individual's goal achievement. Teachers attributed their sense of accountability to the regularity of goal group meetings, the agendas supporting goal work, and the public aspect of their work on goals. The regularity of goal group meetings was important to teachers. Rachel clarified, "The goal group schedule causes you to get on a schedule and stay on a schedule. You have to have that monthly contact."

The collaboratively developed agendas and protocols supported an environment where each teacher had a voice in the strategies of group goals and ownership in the cooperative work during and between meetings. Because the work of the teachers was public, teachers participated because if they had not, it would be evident to their colleagues. These procedures not only promoted accountability but also helped teachers gain a sense of interdependence within the goal group.

The discussions in goal groups were important to teachers because the conversation afforded an opportunity to offer and receive feedback, to see a variety of perspectives, to clarify thinking, and to solidify their own expertise. Emily found that "if you have people to talk it out with, you can start to see the problems or the benefits." Rachel explains that when peers offer feedback to each other, it feels less judgmental and more like refinement or building on an existing idea. Collaborative discussion between teachers can be the strongest predictor of teacher change (Parise & Spillane, 2010). Teachers acknowledge this need for ongoing, sustained communication.

Connecting teachers in collaborative groups across the school also provided opportunities for teachers to find support from teachers outside grade-level teams. Eric valued his goal group work because "it gets you outside of your grade level and it gives you a chance to talk to teachers outside of your grade." Madge said, "It's more than just sharing resources. You learn things from other grade levels that you normally wouldn't get to see or talk about." The purposeful act of creating cross-grade groups of teachers based on goals led to teachers feeling less isolated and more connected to their fellow teachers.

Positive Shifts in School Culture

According to Avalos (2011), professional learning creates positive changes in school culture "due to four main characteristics: collaboration, a focus on student learning, teacher authority described as the ability of teachers to make decisions within their communities, and finally recognition of the importance of teacher continuous learning" (p. 17). The development of teacher networks connected through cross-grade collaboration helped shape and reshape the culture of this elementary school.

Through goal groups, teachers worked in concert with peers to learn. When professionals work together to improve practice, both the individual and the group improve. Halle explained, "We are all doing one thing together," and Lisa said, "We're sharing what we've figured out and whether it worked out or not." Teachers participating in job-embedded, authentic activities are better positioned to implement learning in the classroom. Rachel found that "in goal groups you're learning through experience in your school. You're learning by discussing, and you're learning by participating, and you're learning as you work with students."

When all of the key players within a school—individual teachers, formal groups of teachers, students, and the administrative team—work

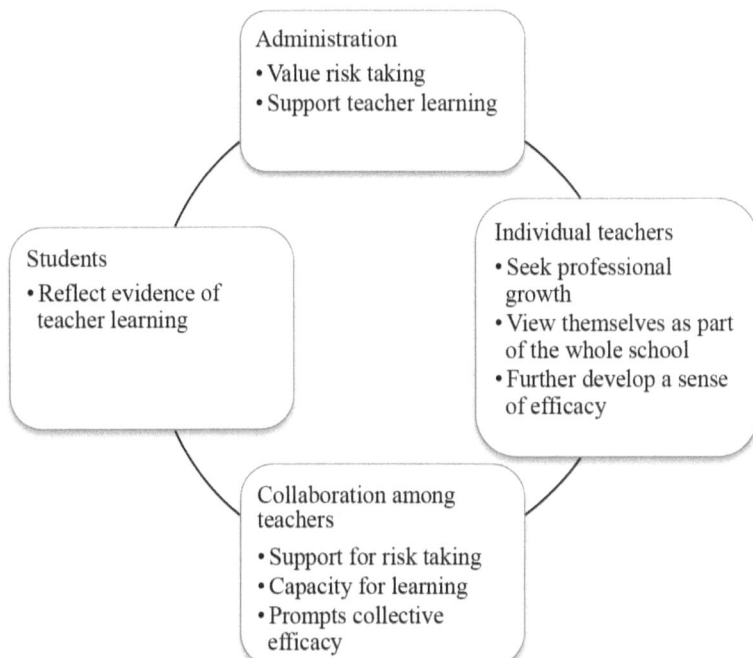

Figure 3.2 Cycle of Influence on Positive School Culture Related to Goal Groups

collaboratively, the culture of the school begins to change. According to Fullan (2011), a culture for school improvement includes a focus on facilitating purposeful interaction where teachers are building capacity when learning while they work. Figure 3.2 illustrates the role of each entity in the cycle of improving school culture in relationship to goal group professional learning. In this cycle, the individual teacher is improving as well as the groups of teachers.

Teachers felt empowered to share learning and to make decisions. Lisa explained, "So if you're in an environment [where everyone is] more open and willing to grow, that makes for a more positive experience as a whole, and sharing what we've figured out makes us a stronger school."

Synergy Propels Learning

A cycle of learning is built into goal group professional learning: individual and collaborative learning, implementing that learning in classrooms, and then reflecting on that implementation. The importance of this cycle to teacher learning was articulated by Eric:

> I would say each step in my group and on my own depends on the other. If I get an idea, I take it to my goal group and I incorporate it in my teaching. Then I take it back to my goal group and say, Hey, this worked, this didn't work, and then I go back and rethink the process all over again, I think it's all interconnected.

This sentiment exemplifies how the individual and collaborative learning in which teachers engage created synergy within goal groups. Viewed through the lens of communal constructivism, teachers created knowledge both for themselves and for their group as they participated in a cycle of learning, implementation, and reflection. The synergic outcomes related to goal groups offered teachers peer support to take risks, built capacity for learning, accelerated the spread of instructional knowledge, and developed teacher networks beyond goal groups.

When teachers had opportunities to solve problems collaboratively and had access to the necessary resources, they were more likely to take risks, persevere to make change, and develop, adapt, and apply ways to support student learning in their classrooms. Madge explained, "If I try something and fall flat, it's going to be okay. Because we are working together, I can go back to my group and get it figured out." The mindset for teachers became a "just try it" way of thinking. Through collaborative experiences in goal groups, teachers developed a greater willingness to take risks.

Gallimore et al. (2009) found that when "teachers slow down and make planning and analysis visible in a collective and intentional way this affects general patterns of cognition," leading to "greater interest in gaining more knowledge about practice and alternative approaches" (p. 549). Exposure to multiple perspectives develops openness to new ideas. Emily explained that she benefited from "being able to see what teachers in other grades do that I wouldn't have any idea about." Teachers revealed the need to be "open to ideas presented." Beth explained, "Goal groups provided me with a group of people as resources to help me develop new ideas." Teachers were empowered to generate ideas and to make instructional decisions.

The synergy that originates in goal groups is a complex blend of organizational structures, self-direction, collaboration, positive learning, and support for implementation. Put together, it gives individuals, groups, and the school community the power to sustain learning over time.

Coherence

The school district teacher evaluation system was founded on a theoretical model of coherence developed by Zepeda (2017). This model of coherence links goal setting, supervision, professional development, and teacher evaluation. Goal group professional learning contextualizes the peer support and teacher learning described in Zepeda's (2017) coherence model.

Goal groups provided a space where teachers worked together around their particular interests or needs. Madge clarified the importance of self-selection of goals when she stated, "I do think we are stronger in our commitment to our goals if we pick them. Giving us the choice makes it more positive and more motivating." Emily said, "I like that I know that other people have a common goal and they're working towards the same thing I am." Emily went on to say that "if you have people to talk it out with, you can start to see the problems or the benefits."

Goal groups created a path that supported teachers' journey from goal setting as a part of evaluation through differentiated professional learning to the end-of-year evaluation. Not only were teachers prepared to meet with the administrator at the end of the year, they also more importantly recognized and celebrated their own learning facilitated through goal group professional learning. The process of goal groups tied together the goal, professional learning, and teacher change in the final evaluation. In other words, this program supported teacher growth and development as much as the evaluation system was designed to do.

Changes in Practice—Changes in Beliefs

Professional development enhances teacher knowledge and improves instructional practice when it connects to teacher's work with students, is sustained over time, links to concrete tasks of teaching, and creates opportunities for collaborative learning from peers that builds strong working relationships (Darling-Hammond et al., 2009). Teachers reported implementing learning from goal groups in their teaching. The changes teachers made in their classrooms surfaced in several places within the data. Table 3.2 presents teachers' reflections on changes in instructional practice. Alex explained, "I definitely think that working on the goal that I worked on impacted the way that I taught and the amount of learning that happened."

Teachers who had participated in goal groups in previous years additionally provided examples of how the previous years' goal group work continued to have an influence on their teaching. Teachers not only made lasting changes in their teaching practice, they also made changes in their beliefs about teaching.

Rachel gave an example of long-term change made through her work in goal groups from previous years. Rachel explained how she used to stand in front of the classroom with all of the desks in rows and "talk at the students." Now Rachel has students sitting in groups, sits down with students in small

Table 3.2 Goal Group Meeting Responses to "I used to . . . but now I . . ."

Goal Group Meeting Reflection Activity
Examples of Responses to "I used to . . . but now I . . ."

- I used to think using technology meant showing my lessons on the smart board. Now my students are completely engaged in technology on their own devices both collaboratively and individually. They have really taken charge of their learning.
- Before I started working on my goal, I did more teacher-centered instruction. Now I engage students more through student-centered activities and frequent checks for understanding.
- I used to assess students and not really use the data to target student need. Now I am able to assess students and know exactly what to teach them.
- Before I started working on my goal, I used to become frustrated with students who had a hard time following classroom routines. Now I realize it was because of how I was directing them. I have learned that I need to be clearer with my directions.

group instruction, and checks for student understanding during the lesson. In talking about this change in her practice, Rachel stated, "It's a big deal."

The changes Rachel made are not only about what she does with students. These changes are indicative of a change in what she believes about teaching. She said, "I used to believe my job was to stand up there and tell the students what to learn. If they didn't get it, it wasn't my fault." Now she believed her job was about developing relationships with students and making sure students were learning. Rachel explained, "It's not simple. Teaching is much more three dimensional than I thought." The teacher has to interact in meaningful ways with the students to ensure that student learning is happening. Rachel described it this way: "I've become more observant and responsive to students." Rachel has a new understanding of what it means to be a teacher.

IMPLICATIONS FOR SCHOOL LEADERS

Findings from this study hold promise as a guide for school leaders and professional developers interested in improving student outcomes. Darling-Hammond et al. (2009) reported, "Efforts to improve student achievement can succeed only by building the capacity of teachers to improve their instructional practice and the capacity of school systems to promote teacher learning" (p. 7). Professional learning needs to honor teachers' ability to self-select learning through goal setting and to engage in appropriate professional learning that responds to the real needs of teachers in the school setting.

For the principal, teacher evaluation happens every year. The goal group process emanates from initial teacher evaluation meetings when administrators and teachers discuss teacher goal setting at the beginning of the school year. The goals set by teachers drive a major portion of the school-level professional learning plan for the year. This professional learning for teachers creates a connection between goals and evaluation.

From a principal or building leader's perspective, facilitating the goal group process with or without an instructional coach requires minimal time and effort beyond what is already required as a part of teacher evaluation. Building leaders initially coordinate groups then make the time and space for teachers to meet seven or eight times a year. The remainder of the planning and work is left to the teachers.

This minimal effort is worth its potential benefit to administrators. If supervision is meant to improve teaching and learning, here is a process that seamlessly connects supervision, professional learning, and evaluation. As goal setting is part of many evaluation systems, instead of teachers working toward goal attainment individually, they work collaboratively in groups. The goal group process supports teacher accountability and supports an overall teacher evaluation system as teachers document work toward expectations. In the ongoing debate over teacher evaluation tied to accountability, goal group professional learning is a model that codifies the relationships between supervision, teacher learning, and evaluation.

SUMMARY

Practitioners considering similar reform efforts must take steps to ensure that goal groups are actualized in an effective fashion. The district under study established the conditions necessary to support a teacher evaluation system predicated on a growth model. The teacher was at the center of the evaluation and situated as the learner in an effort to improve instructional practices based on teacher professional standards. School administrators must subscribe to the premise that the purpose of teacher evaluation is to improve teacher practice and support teacher learning. Goal groups can support this type of development.

Discussion Questions
1. Think about your beliefs regarding teachers driving the content of professional learning. How do you create coherence between teacher supervision and teacher professional learning?
2. As a leader, what would your next steps be toward moving your school to goal-based, job-embedded professional learning?
3. How might teachers show evidence of learning related to goal-based, job-embedded professional learning?

SUGGESTED READINGS

DuFour, R., Eaker, R., Many, T. W., & Mattos, M. (2016). *Learning by doing: A handbook for professional learning communities at work* (3rd ed.). Bloomington, IN: Solution Tree Press.
Fullan, M., Quinn, J., & Adam, E. (2016). *The taking action guide to building coherence in schools, districts, and systems.* Thousand Oaks, CA: Corwin.
Zepeda, S. J. (2014) *The principal as instructional leader: A handbook for supervisors* (3rd. ed.). New York, NY: Routledge.

REFERENCES

Avalos, B. (2011). Teacher professional development in *Teaching and Teacher Education* over ten years. *Teaching and Teacher Education, 27*(1), 10–20. http://dx.doi.org/10.1016/j.tate.2010.08.007
Bayar, A. (2014). The components of effective professional development activities in terms of teachers' perspective. *International Online Journal of Educational Sciences, 6*(2), 319–327. http://dx.doi.org/10.15345/iojes.2014.02.006
Brookfield, S. D. (2013). *Powerful techniques for teaching adults.* San Francisco, CA: Jossey-Bass.
Croft, A., Coggshall, J. G., Dolan, M., & Powers, E. (2010). Job-embedded professional development: What it is, who is responsible, and how to get it done well. Issue Brief. *National Comprehensive Center for Teacher Quality.* Retrieved from http://ncctq.org/
Darling-Hammond, L. (2010). Teacher education and the American future. *Journal of Teacher Education, 61*(1–2), 35–47. http://dx.doi.org/10.1177/0022487109348024
Darling-Hammond, L., & McLaughlin, M. W. (2011). Policies that support professional development in an era of reform. *Phi Delta Kappan, 92*(6), 81–92. http://dx.doi.org/10.1177/003172171109200622
Darling-Hammond, L., Wei, R. C., Andree, A., Richardson, N., & Orphanos, S. (2009). *Professional learning in the learning profession: A status report on teacher development in the United States and abroad.* Dallas, TX: National Staff Development Council. Retrieved from http://learningforward.org/docs/pdf/nsdcstudy2009.pdf
Desimone, L. M. (2011). A primer on effective professional development. *Phi Delta Kappan, 92*(6), 68–71. http://dx.doi.org/10.1177/003172171109200616
Fullan, M. (2011). *The six secrets of change: What the best leaders do to help their organizations survive and thrive.* Hoboken, NJ: John Wiley & Sons.
Gallimore, R., Ermeling, B. A., Saunders, W. M., & Goldenberg, C. (2009). Moving the learning of teaching closer to practice: Teacher education implications of school-based inquiry teams. *Elementary School Journal, 109*(5), 537–553. http://dx.doi.org/10.1086/597001
Glickman, C. D., Gordon, S. P., & Ross-Gordon, J. M. (2012). *The basic guide to supervision and instructional leadership.* Boston, MA: Pearson Higher Education.

Grant, A. M. (2012). An integrated model of goal-focused coaching: An evidence-based framework for teaching and practice. *International Coaching Psychology Review*, 7(2), 146–165. Retrieved from http://www.sgcp.org.uk/

Guskey, T. R. (2011). Evaluation: Critical to professional development. *Principal Matters*, 87(1), 44–48. Retrieved from http://www.awsp.org/news/publications/principalmatters

Hamilton, L., & Whittier, C. (2013). *Using case study in education research*. Thousand Oaks, CA: Sage Publications.

Harris, D. N., & Sass, T. R. (2011). Teacher training, teacher quality, and student achievement. *Journal of Public Economics*, 95(7), 798–812. http://dx.doi.org/10.1016/j.jpubeco.2010.11.009

Hirsh, S. (2009). A new definition. *Journal of Staff Development*, 30(4), 10–16. Retrieved from http://www.nsdc.org

Hord, S. M. (2009). Professional learning communities: Educators work together toward a shared purpose. *Journal of Staff Development*, 30(1), 40–43. Retrieved from http://www.nsdc.org

Johnson, D. W., Johnson, R. T., & Smith, K. (2007). The state of cooperative learning in postsecondary and professional settings. *Educational Psychology Review*, 19(1), 15–29. http://dx.doi.org/10.1007/s10648-006-9038-8

Locke, E. A., & Latham, G. P. (Eds.). (2013). *New developments in goal setting and task performance*. New York, NY: Routledge.

Parise, L. M., & Spillane, J. P. (2010). Teacher learning and instructional change: How formal and on-the-job learning opportunities predict change in elementary school teachers' practice. *Elementary School Journal*, 110(3), 323–346. http://dx.doi.org/10.1086/648981

Parker, S. L., Jimmieson, N. L., & Amiot, C. E. (2009). The stress-buffering effects of control on task satisfaction and perceived goal attainment: An experimental study of the moderating influence of desire for control. *Applied Psychology*, 58(4), 622–652. http://dx.doi.org/10.1111/j.1464-0597.2008.00367.x

Schwandt, T. A. (2007). *The Sage dictionary of qualitative inquiry* (3rd ed.). Thousand Oaks, CA: Sage Publications.

Slavin, R. E. (2014). Cooperative learning and academic achievement: Why does groupwork work? *Anales De Psicología*, 30(3), 785–791. http://dx.doi.org/10.6018/analesps.30.3.201201

Sparks, D. (2013). Strong teams, strong schools. *Journal of Staff Development*, 34(2), 28–30. Retrieved from http://learningforward.org/

Whitfield, B. L., & Wood, D. R. (2010). *Teachers learning in community: Realities and possibilities*. Albany: State University of New York Press.

Zepeda, S. J. (2012). *Professional development: What works* (2nd ed.). New York, NY: Routledge.

Zepeda, S. J. (2017). *Instructional supervision: Applying tools and concepts* (4th ed.). New York, NY: Routledge.

Chapter 4

The Impact of Incoherent Professional Learning on Standards-Based Reform

Michael P. Cassidy

SCENARIO

Nicole walks into the teacher lounge, pulls out a chair at the table, and sits down very frustrated. Terry is standing at the copier running off worksheets for a substitute. She asks, "Something wrong?"

"I have to go another stupid professional learning seminar tomorrow. It's such a waste of time," Nicole answers.

"Yea, I know. I'm going too. Apparently, we're going to learn some new Research-Based Extraneous Strategy that the district thinks will improve all test scores."

"I think it'll even make the kids taller too." Both enjoy the joke for a second. Nicole continues, "But I don't think the district gets it. They get people from God knows where to teach us how to do something new."

"Even if it contradicts what we were told to do the week before."

"I know right. The district knows it's a joke. That's why they don't even follow up to see if you're doing it. But we still have to go."

Terry adds, "The district is just trying to please whatever initiative the state has adopted to get extra money from the federal government. The problem is our legislators have no idea what the hell's going on in our classrooms."

"Yep. But if we go to professional learning about anything and everything, we'll fix all society's problems. This is such a joke." She gathers her things and gets up, "See you tomorrow, Terry."

"Save me a seat."

KEY IDEAS IN THIS CHAPTER

- Coherence begins with district and school leaders consistently offering professional learning about standards and initiatives that are being implemented in classrooms.
- Teachers' professional learning must align with standards, curriculum, and professional needs.
- Professional learning should promote and develop teacher agency.

ABSTRACT

This chapter explores middle school science teachers' (1) knowledge of the Common Core State Standards, (2) literacy-related professional learning experiences, and (3) implementation of literacy instructional practices. Teachers' perspectives revealed their professional learning activities lacked coherence between standards, instructional practices, and professional needs. To promote coherence, developing teacher agency is suggested.

INTRODUCTION

Educational reform policies increasingly target teacher professional learning as integral to improved student achievement (Bickmore, 2013). More specifically, coherent approaches to professional learning are identified as a crucial component for implementation of successful, standards-based reform. To promote coherence, standards, curriculum, and teacher professional learning need to align (National Research Council, 2012; Penuel, Fishman, Gallagher, Korbak, & Lopez-Prado, 2009; Reiser, 2014). Therefore, there is a need to understand the types of professional learning teachers engage in while implementing new standards.

This study examined middle school science teachers' perspectives on their professional learning as they implemented the Common Core State Standards for literacy in science. Teachers' perspectives on their professional learning are the focus of this chapter. During this study, science standards–based reform was underway as states were deciding whether to adopt the Common Core or Next Generation Science Standards (NGSS Lead States, 2013). As context for this study, the state and school district had adopted the Common Core, but both were unsure about adopting Next Gen.

The chapter begins with an overview of the literature followed by context, research methods, and findings. The chapter ends with implications for school leaders, discussion questions, and suggested readings.

OVERVIEW OF THE LITERATURE

The overview of literature begins with a description the Common Core and Next Gen—specifically, their impact on literacy classroom instruction. This literature provides an important background for examining teachers' perspectives on their professional learning while implementing the Common Core for literacy in science.

Common Core State Standards and Next Generation Science Standards

Beginning in 1994 with the reauthorization of the Elementary and Secondary Education Act, standards-based reform became common practice (Goals 2000, 1994). Fast forward nearly a decade, the No Child Left Behind Act of 2001 promised all students would be 100% proficient in reading and mathematics by 2014 (U.S. Congress, 2001). These lofty goals were not met. In fact, the American public realized they were well behind many of their international peers in science, reading, and mathematics (Goldstein, 2014). The American people believed students were not being prepared to be successful in college or for career entry. In response, the Common Core was launched in 2009, and Next Gen was released in 2013.

The Common Core was created by the National Governors Association Center for Best Practices and the Council of Chief State School Officers. The standards were set for grades kindergarten through 12 in the areas of mathematics, English language arts, and literacy in science, social studies, and technical subjects. The purpose of the Common Core is "to provide a consistent, clear understanding of what students are expected to learn so teachers and parents know what they need to do to help them" (Common Core State Standards Initiative [Common Core], 2015a, para. 3) at each grade level. For literacy in science standards, students are expected to be able to read, write, and speak about specific content matter.

The standards are designed to help young people develop knowledge and skills that will help them in their future college and career endeavors (Kendall, 2011). The Common Core is meant to position U.S. students to compete in a global economy (Common Core, 2015b). Through professional learning support for teachers and school leaders, the Common Core is expected to influence student learning and achievement (Achieve, 2013).

Currently, 42 states, the District of Columbia, and the Department of Defense Education Activity have adopted the Common Core (Common Core, 2015c).

Because of a lack of focus on science content standards in the Common Core, several organizations began to develop Next Gen. The organizations that collaboratively developed Next Gen include the National Research Council, the National Science Teachers Association, the American Association for the Advancement of Science, and a nonprofit education organization called Achieve. These organizations took a two-step approach to develop Next Gen.

First, the developers defined a vision for science education in the 21st century and articulated what students need to know in each grade to be considered scientifically literate. The vision included a learning progression of core ideas (specific content and subject areas), scientific and engineering practices (understanding science content and scientific methods), and cross-cutting ideas (underlying ideas that are common among science concepts) that integrate various disciplines of science.

After this vision for science education had been developed, the second step was to invite all states to develop student performance expectations for each grade level, but only 26 states participated (Pruitt, 2014). Like the Common Core, Next Gen aimed to prepare students for college and careers.

Moreover, Next Gen contains eight scientific and engineering practices that define inquiry for science classroom practices (Spencer & Bouwma-Gearhart, 2014). Of the eight scientific and engineering practices, four are language-intensive to promote sensemaking practices that engage learners in

- developing and using models;
- constructing explanations (for science) and designing solutions (for engineering);
- engaging in argument from evidence; and
- obtaining, evaluating, and communicating information. (Hakuta, Santos, & Fang, 2013, p. 453)

Currently, 40 states have shown interest in the standards, and 18 states and the District of Columbia have adopted Next Gen.

To clarify, there is a difference between the Common Core for literacy in science and being scientifically literate as promoted by Next Gen. The Common Core for literacy in science for middle school is integrated with English language arts standards. For example, students need to be able to cite specific textual evidence to support analysis of science and technical subjects. Therefore, middle school science teachers need to teach students how to engage in argumentation and to read and write expository essays. Being scientifically literate means one has a knowledge of broad scientific concepts that can be applied to societal issues and concerns (Bybee, 2014).

Research has addressed teaching science and literacy at various grade levels. For example, in elementary classrooms, studies report the effectiveness of teaching science content and literacy skills side by side (Carrejo & Reinhartz, 2012). In secondary classrooms, students are expected to read science-specific texts more fully, but they receive little explicit reading instruction (Tong, Irby, Lara-Alecio, & Koch, 2014). Middle school students rarely receive explicit literacy instruction in science classrooms (Greenleaf et al., 2011). Lee, Quinn, and Valdés (2013) emphasize the importance for middle school science teachers' lessons of focusing on the language-rich aspects of inquiry and communication embedded in scientific practices.

Unfortunately, studies of professional learning pertaining to the Common Core for literacy in science classrooms are scarce (Jagger & Yore, 2012). Most of the science-literacy related professional learning studies concentrate on implementing inquiry-based instruction, prospective science teachers, English language learners, and implementing science-literacy units (Capps, Crawford, & Constas, 2012; Cervetti, Barber, Droph, Pearson, & Goldschmidt, 2012).

Professional Learning

Zepeda (2015) defined professional learning as "learning for students, teachers, and other professionals who support children" (p. 2). Successful professional learning practices involve people working to improve curriculum, instructional practices, and student assessments to make student growth possible (Gordon, 2004). Teacher professional learning needs to be embedded in the culture of the school as day-to-day work rather than as an add-on to the day (Zepeda, 2015). Professional learning should spark curiosity, motivation, and new ways of thinking.

Historically, research into the implementation of standards shows teachers need high-quality professional learning (Coburn, Hill, & Spillane, 2016). Over the years, studies of professional learning (Desimone, 2009; Zepeda, 2012) have identified key aspects of effective and useful programs that

- extend over time and allow teachers sufficient time to interact with resources;
- are continuous and ongoing, with planned follow-up;
- are content- and grade-specific to teachers' subject matter;
- promote collaboration, brainstorming, reflection, and inquiry;
- provide various learning strategies;
- use student data to frame and assess learning needs;
- are evaluated and assessed on an ongoing basis;
- are embedded in the workday and relevant to teacher needs; and

- are coherent with state standards, school policies, and practices.

Job-embedded professional development takes place when "teacher learning is grounded in day-to-day teaching practice and is designed to enhance teachers' content-specific instructional practices with the intent of improving student learning" (Croft, Coggshall, Dolan, Powers, & Killion, 2010, p. 2). There are five characteristics of job-embedded learning:

- hold relevance for the adult learner (because adults want to be successful and derive value from their learning, job-embedded learning is highly individualized);
- include feedback as part of the process (job-embedded learning includes feedback and collaborative supports as a built-in process—for example, peer coaching);
- support inquiry and reflection (job-embedded learning promotes thinking more critically and reflectively about practice at an individual or group level);
- facilitate the transfer of new skills into practice (job-embedded learning provides ongoing support, which is linked to transferring learned skills into practice); and
- promote collaboration (through collaboration, teachers share with one another, engage in discussions, and reflect on their experiences). (Zepeda, 2015, pp. 35–38)

For job-embedded professional learning to be at its best, teachers must learn to trust each other and to work well in teams. Furthermore, professional learning that is job-embedded provides an opportunity for state standards and initiatives to cohere with professional learning and teacher instruction.

"Coherence" means professional learning is "consistent with the participants' knowledge and beliefs and its connectedness, including conflicts and tensions, as well as the relationship of the content of that which is delivered to school, district, and state reforms and policies, standards, curriculum and assessment" (Waring, 2016, p. 296). Firestone, Mangin, Martinez, and Polovsky (2005) proposed three ways to establish coherence:

- focus on fewer topics to establish more in-depth knowledge;
- allow time to try new materials and ideas, and reflect and refine them; and
- model the instructional approaches that teachers are expected to employ (p. 416).

To promote coherence, district leaders have the potential to play an enormous role in improving teacher and student learning. District leaders, specifically content coaches, often mediate between what teachers need and what a school district requires (Durand, Lawson, Wilcox, & Schiller, 2016). Content coaches often support teachers by creating and implementing professional learning opportunities. Typically, content coaches interpret new policies and initiatives by introducing and often modeling new instructional strategies. Therefore, it is imperative they have in-depth knowledge of standards in order to communicate expectations clearly to teachers (Whitworth, Maeng, Wheeler, & Chiu, 2017).

CONTEXT OF THE STUDY

For this study, the state and district fully adopted the Common Core while remaining unsure about adopting Next Gen. The school simultaneously implemented multiple other initiatives such as one-to-one technology and new assessments for teachers and students. Teachers received professional learning from the district science coach while the professional learning related to the other initiative came from school or system administrators.

The study took place in a small, urban middle school in a southern town. The school serves a population of nearly 700 students in grades 6 through 8. The free and reduced lunch rate is about 80%, qualifying the middle school as a Title I school—typical demographics for the district.

Five science teachers participated in this study. They brought a combination of over 40 years of middle school science teaching experience. Four out of the five participants had advanced degrees. Two were female and three were male. The teachers and the researcher agreed that all study participants would remain anonymous.

RESEARCH METHODS

This study employs a case study methodology (Creswell, 2013) and applies the constant comparative method (Corbin & Strauss, 2015) for analysis to examine the teachers' perspectives on their professional learning as they implemented the Common Core for literacy in science. Data were collected over a six-month period and included

- two semi-structured interviews that each lasted approximately 45 minutes with each participant, totaling 10 interviews;
- field notes recording formal and informal discussions pertaining to literacy instruction from shadowing participants during 14 science department meetings; and

- artifacts such as agendas and meeting notes to help paint a fuller picture of the case study and corroborate information from other sources.

Data analysis was an iterative, inductive process in which the data were read holistically, codes were developed, and memos were written. After the memos were completed, tables were created systematically to organize the data, show relationships, and integrate ideas about the data. Throughout this process, the constant comparative method supported the development of categories and themes (Charmaz, 2000).

FINDINGS

All participants discussed their perspectives on their professional learning as they implemented the Common Core for literacy in science. The themes that emerged from the data included (1) insufficient knowledge of standards, (2) inconsistent professional learning activities, and (3) inapplicable instructional strategies.

Theme One: Insufficient Knowledge of Standards

Participants in this study relied heavily on district and school leaders to tell them what they needed to teach. More specifically, the science content coach played an important role in the teachers' understanding of the standards. One participant explained, "[The district] provides professional learning based on new things being passed in legislation [e.g., new student assessments]." Another teacher added, "[The science coach] basically funnels information, reiterates what is coming down, you know, what is being introduced to the legislature and that trickles down to what we need to teach." This was where the lack of coherence began.

The state adopted the Common Core and not Next Gen. However, there was much discussion among the teachers about which standards should be taught in their classroom. One participant's knowledge of the standards came straight from the content coach: "The Common Core really doesn't affect science [in our district] . . . there is a big push toward the Next Generation Science Standards by the science coach." Another teacher said, "Next Gen is kind of our Common Core." Both teachers believed Next Gen was being implemented in classrooms. In addition, one teacher attended a regional conference funded by the district for Next Gen instructional strategies.

The idea that Next Gen should be taught was not endorsed by all. One teacher claimed, "I do not pay attention to the Next Generation Science Standards because a lot of people don't think it's going to go through."

Simply put, the participants were unsure what standards to implement. The science coach did not clearly convey information to the teachers about the standards, and this lack of clarity created more uncertainty.

Confusion about the standards continued when the participants discussed the Common Core for literacy in science. For example, one teacher admitted, "I have not really read them through completely so I'm not sure what applies . . . I don't see them enough." Another participant added, "Ah, to be blatantly honest I really don't think about those things. I just come into the room and teach." Other attitudes toward the standards included "Teaching is just teaching. It comes to me naturally" and "I just make sure I teach what I am supposed to teach." These types of statements beg the question, how do teachers know what to teach if they were unaware of what state standards are being implemented?

To help mitigate this issue, the school district created a curriculum portal with lists of activities and assessments to go along with a pacing guide for teachers. To create the curriculum portal, district coaches and content leaders developed units. But in the portal, teachers claimed they did not see literacy standards. For example, one teacher explained that the portal included "the characteristics we teach, like habits of mind, analyzing tables and graphs, stuff like that." Although the teachers rarely discussed the standards or saw them, they all recognized there was more of a focus by the school on including more reading instruction in their classrooms. For help with literacy instructional strategies, they attended professional learning activities.

Theme Two: Inconsistent Professional Learning Activities

A lack of knowledge about standards emerged largely because the science content coach conveyed an unclear message. This resulted in teachers being uncertain which standards to implement. In this section, inconsistent professional learning activities further highlight incoherence while implementing new standards.

For the teachers in this study, their inconsistent professional learning activities led to a stressful and frustrating frame of mind. All the teachers said they had "lots of professional learning opportunities." District-wide professional learning occurred at the beginning and end of the school year. During the school year, teachers met twice a week for grade or content meetings. In addition, they attended weekly Working on Work meetings. These meetings were led by teachers or instructional coaches. The study participants also attended professional learning sessions related to technology, assessments, teacher evaluations, and literacy instruction as part of a recently awarded grant.

The amount of professional learning opportunities teachers received led to negative feelings. One participant disclosed, "Sometimes I think [professional learning] is too much because it seems that is all you do. You know, I want to do work in my room." Another teacher admitted that all the professional learning became "overkill" because it was "too much," and teachers were not given enough time to "digest" what was learned. Therefore, "it stresses me out." Others agreed and felt there was "too much being thrown at them at once." According to one participant, it was "a waste of time . . . [because all the different activities make] too many things go on in my head."

The participants had a difficult time recalling literacy-related professional learning apart from a reading strategy. All recalled PALs Reading, a partner reading strategy, because it was "mentioned a lot in meetings." This strategy resonated with teachers because they asked the administration for more training. This request led to an English language arts teacher filming a PALS Reading lesson to use as an example of how to implement the strategy.

As for writing and vocabulary strategies, teachers saw no benefit in their literacy-related professional learning. For example, one teacher, recalling a writing strategy, said, "We had one at the beginning of the year . . . but I don't remember it." Another teacher disclosed, "The strategy was too long . . . He taught us to write a complete paper . . . We don't need that long of writing for science."

For vocabulary, one teacher could not recall the strategy but believed it "was a good one" although it was "not efficient in terms of what they want us to do in addition to [other] initiatives." Another participant confessed, "I have not received professional learning on teaching vocabulary."

Besides PALs Reading, there was little follow-up from the district on any initiative or, specifically, literacy instruction. One participant said, "The district only checks data. They never check whether we [are] teaching a strategy." Another teacher said most professional learning was "one and done unless we specify to [the school administration] that we need more." There was so little follow-up to these strategies that one participant at the end of the school year stated the last literacy-related Working on Work meeting was "light years ago."

More frustration for the teachers piled up when they viewed professional learning as not related to their content. One teacher said, "We do a lot of literacy like PALs, but every time I go, it's kind of disappointing. It's always about ELA . . . all of it was focused 100% on ELA." Another participant said, "When it is about ELA, I block it out . . . they don't show me how to use it for my subject." When teachers received literacy-related professional learning, they did not view it as related to their content. In fact, another teacher admitted, "Content is the one thing we don't get enough of . . . [the district] is probably still trying figure out that balance of professional learning" to implement all the initiatives.

The district and school leaders provided an opportunity for teachers to make their professional learning more personal through a suggestion box. All participants believed that the administration recognized their input. However, none of the participants took advantage of this opportunity. One participant wished they could pick their own activities "and not be told what to do." Another said in frustration, "After all these sessions that make no hill of beans to us . . . and they ask is there anything you want to see? I'm like nope . . . We're meeting'd out because it is inapplicable stuff."

Theme Three: Inapplicable Instructional Strategies

For the teachers in this study, they did not think any of the instructional strategies presented during their professional learning were suitable for their students. For example, one teacher recalled an experience they "blocked out" because it was a demonstration of a classroom with "some teacher from Texas that has 95% perfect scores." The teacher said it was a great strategy for that Texas classroom, but the strategy was "not going to work for my kid who can't write very well." Another reason why teachers did not implement specific strategies was that they were "too time-consuming."

The PALs Reading strategy was the exception. Because of all the professional learning received, PALS Reading became their "bread and butter for reading assignments." That said, teachers were hesitant at first because they thought it might be "too elementary" for their middle school students. Once the teachers saw "the kids really enjoying it, then [they] used it a lot." PALs Reading instruction satisfied the grant received. Another reading strategy used often was call-and-response questioning for comprehension while reading to the whole class.

Instead of using a strategy that was viewed as being "all about ELA," teachers tried strategies they learned via Google or Pinterest. For writing instruction, one teacher explained, "I made up a writing strategy to be honest with you . . . I don't think it is research-based, but I saw kids struggling." The teacher admitted, "The strategy is really just restating the question . . . this way they get some points on [the new assessment]." Assessment-driven literacy instruction was common practice. Another teacher commented, "I have them complete constructive responses a lot because it is on [the new assessment]." Other writing instruction included referencing the various forms of the verb "to be" written on the chalkboard and having students "write song lyrics or a poem" about a topic.

Because of a lack of classroom time, vocabulary strategies suggested were not used either. Teachers instead reviewed terms quickly with students. One teacher claimed to "do the key words while reading a chapter, but it took up so much time. There is so much content to cover." This teacher said, "So we focus on what [the students] are having the hardest time with and provide a real-life example." Another explained, "It is best to use those terms in class, in the hallway, at lunch . . . I don't want my kids to think it is a big fancy science word . . . I just use it when we speak and it naturally sticks." Providing real-world examples was important to the teachers because the vocabulary was "like teaching a foreign language" to their students.

One teacher was the exception when it came to literacy-related professional learning and instruction. The teacher admitted going to a regional Next Gen conference. This participant described multiple techniques used in the classroom. For example, to teach vocabulary, this teacher introduced a new concept by allowing students to first do an experimental lab and explore before going over the vocabulary. The teacher did this because it was "one of the concepts behind the Next Gen. We let the kids explore and discover on their own."

DISCUSSION OF FINDINGS

In this research, teachers shared perspectives on their professional learning as they implemented the Common Core for science in literacy. The results highlight why standards, professional learning, and teacher instruction need to be coherent. Teachers were uncertain of which standards they were to implement because of poor communication with district leaders. As a result, their professional learning was not aligned coherently with standards. Because of poor professional learning experiences, teachers improvised their literacy instructional practices.

Kaufman, Thompson, and Opfer (2016) discussed the importance of creating a coherent system to support instruction aligned with state standards, and they summarized, "If teachers do not deeply understand their standards—or the instructional practices that are aligned with them—their instruction may fall short of helping students meet those standards" (p. 7). Furthermore, Coburn's 2004 study of reading reforms showed teachers' interpretations of policy messages influenced their instructional practices related to the reform.

In this study, teachers did not fully understand the state standards that were being implemented. Therefore, teachers' interpretations of the standards-based reform were contradictory. The science coach was the primary support for the teachers and made decisions regarding professional learning and the design of science curricula. Because the science coach did not carry out the state plan to implement the Common Core, educational change was impeded (Johnson, 2013).

Misinformation about standards leads to teachers not receiving professional learning that supports the educational goals of the state. Teachers in this study did not receive subject-oriented professional learning to further their science knowledge or their science-literacy knowledge. In fact, content-related professional learning was the one thing they didn't "get enough of," and their literacy-related professional learning was "all about ELA."

Teacher instructional practices reflected their interpretation of the standards and professional learning experiences. Most of the teachers did not think the standards or their professional learning related to their subject or students. Therefore, teachers' literacy instructional practices did not reflect the goals of the district. Teachers came up with their own strategies to teach literacy skills. While many tried to teach reading, writing, and vocabulary, others admitted "not having enough time," as a result, to teach to the test.

The findings here are a cautionary tale about incoherence between standards awareness, professional learning, and teacher instructional practices. Large-scale reforms such as the implementation of new standards requires coherence between the state, the district, the schools, and the classrooms (National Research Council, 2012). Otherwise, intended student outcomes will not occur (Johnson, 2013).

This study showed that coherence was missing on all levels. There was no focus on new standards. There was no coherent academic strategy focused on integration of literacy in science classrooms via professional learning (with the exception of PALs Reading). This was apparent from the lack of follow-up and support for teachers by the district. Therefore, teachers did not take ownership of the change needed in their instructional practices because they did not believe the reform affected them.

IMPLICATIONS FOR SCHOOL LEADERS

Championing coherence as a school leader is no easy task. School leaders are responsible for understanding district and state goals then devising a plan to support teachers to achieve the outcomes desired by the district and state. When a state and district adopt multiple initiatives, it can be difficult to focus on only one. But it is up to the school leader to concentrate consistently on a topic and then to allow teachers time to understand what is asked of them.

At this school, the school leader needed to concentrate on implementing the Common Core. The participants repeatedly stated their time was wasted and they had other professional needs. Therefore, school leaders need to look for ways to develop and increase teacher agency. Teacher agency is "the capacity of teachers to act purposefully and constructively to direct their professional growth and contribute to the growth of their colleagues" (Calvert, 2016, p. 4).

Coburn (2006) suggests that the way school leaders frame reform initiatives affects teachers' reactions. Therefore, if school leaders empower teachers to choose their own professional learning, teachers may be more likely to implement a reform with fidelity.

Providing teachers with online professional learning opportunities is an increasingly popular model (Means, Toyama, Murphy, Bakia, & Jones, 2009). Research into online environments for professional learning suggests it may facilitate active learning and collaboration and engage teachers in content-related activities. However, there is little research examining how online professional learning programs align with state, district, and school goals and initiatives (Surrette & Johnson, 2015). If this is the model chosen, there needs to be an evaluation plan to ensure coherence.

Another option is lesson study, which is a type of professional learning that promotes year-long teacher collaboration and inquiry through planning, observing, discussing, and evaluating sessions (Lewis, Perry, & Hurd, 2004). Lesson study professional learning allows teachers to plan and observe a specific lesson and strategy. However, lesson study can be time-consuming.

To help save time, school leaders can explore creating a video library of instructional strategies. Videos can be embedded with specific standards in the curriculum. For example, a teacher can videotape a science lesson using a literacy strategy he or she learned at a conference. The teacher can upload the video, and the other science teachers can watch it at their convenience. Further, the teachers can then provide feedback and have an open dialogue in an asynchronous chatroom (Killion, 2013). As more videos are uploaded to the library, teachers can each choose their professional learning experiences. Additionally, the video library could be monitored, providing school leaders with data about which professional learning topics the teachers explored most.

An emerging option to promote teacher agency and coherence is collaborative design, or co-design (Voogt et al., 2015). This approach can flatten hierarchical traditions of professional learning programs. Instead of a consultant or a school leader leading professional learning, teachers can assume a more participatory approach in their learning. Collaboratively, a team made up of teachers, researchers, and developers can work to design curricular materials. Using an iterative approach, the team designs lessons or strategies, implements them, reflects on the implementation, and then refines the lessons or strategies (Severance, Penuel, Sumner, & Leary, 2016).

To carry out this collaborative, design-based research, the team should use a conjecture mapping approach (Sandoval, 2014). Conjecture maps articulate "the joint design and theoretical ideas embodied in a learning environment in a way that supports choices about the means for testing them" (p. 20). The team first theorizes how learning happens before implementation and predicts and tests learning outcomes, then uses the results to refine the design and theory. Like lesson study, this process is time-consuming.

Changes in standards means changes in classroom practices. Using any of the professional development models suggested, teachers can develop agency.

SUMMARY

The purpose of this study was to examine five middle school science teachers' perspectives on their professional learning as they implemented the Common Core for literacy in science. The study revealed what happens if there is incoherence among state standards, professional learning activities, and classroom instructional practices. Theme one discussed the importance of teachers being knowledgeable of state standards and the important role content coaches play in standards-based reform.

Theme two highlighted that teachers can feel overwhelmed and frustrated if they do not think their professional learning relates to their classroom. Theme three provided examples of classroom instructional practices when teachers are not knowledgeable of standards and are not offered high-quality, professional learning.

The implications for school leaders include three different approaches for developing teacher agency through professional learning. The first suggestion is creating an online environment; however, there is limited research into online programs promoting coherence. Lesson study with a video component is the second suggestion. Finally, collaborative design recommends an iterative, design-based research approach.

Discussion Questions
1. To what extent and in what ways do state standards, professional learning activities, and classroom instruction align at your school?
2. What types of evidence would you cite to demonstrate that teachers integrate literacy instruction in their specific subject area at your school?
3. What does teacher agency look and sound like at your school?

SUGGESTED READINGS

Fullan, M., Quinn, J., & Adam, E. (2016). *The taking action guide to building coherence in schools, districts, and systems.* Thousand Oaks, CA: Corwin.

National Academies of Sciences, Engineering, and Medicine. (2017). *Seeing students learn science: Integrating assessment and instruction in the classroom.* Washington, DC: National Academies Press.

Stosich, E. L., Bocala, C., & Forman, M. (2017). Building coherence for instructional improvement through professional development: A design-based implementation research study. *Educational Management Administration & Leadership, 45*(1), 1–17. doi:10.1177/1741143217711193

REFERENCES

Achieve. (2013). *Closing the expectations gap: 2013 annual report on the alignment of state K–12 policies and practice with the demands of college and careers.* Washington, DC: Achieve.

Bickmore, D. L. (2013). Professional development and the middle school concept: A reciprocal relationship. In P. G. Andrews (Ed.), *Research to guide practice in middle grades education*, (pp. 717–749). Westerville, OH: Association for Middle Level Education.

Bybee, R. W. (2014). NGSS and the next generation of science teachers. *Journal of Science Teacher Education, 25*(2), 211–221. doi:10.1007/s10972-014-9381-4

Calvert, L. (2016). *Moving from compliance to agency: What teachers need to make professional learning work.* Oxford, OH: Learning Forward/NCTAF.

Capps, D. K., Crawford, B. A., & Constas, M. A. (2012). A review of empirical literature on inquiry professional development: Alignment with best practices and a critique of the findings. *Journal of Science Teacher Education, 23*(3), 291–318. doi:10.1007/s10972-012-9275-2

Carrejo, D. J., & Reinhartz, J. (2012). Exploring the synergy between science literacy and language literacy with English language learners: Lessons learned with a sustained professional development program. *SRATE Journal, 21*(2), 33–38. Retrieved from http://srate.org/

Cervetti, G. N., Barber, J., Droph, R., Pearson, P. D., & Goldschmidt, P. G. (2012). The impact of an integrated approach to science and literacy in elementary school classrooms. *Journal of Research in Science Teaching, 49*(5), 631–658. doi:10.1002/tea.21015

Charmaz, K. (2000). Constructivist and objectivist grounded theory. In N. K. Denzin & Y. S. Lincoln (Eds.), *Handbook of Qualitative Research* (2nd ed.) (pp. 509–535). Thousand Oaks, CA: Sage Publications.

Coburn, C. E. (2004). Beyond decoupling: Rethinking the relationship between the institutional environment and the classroom. *Sociology of Education, 77*(3), 211–244. doi:10.1177/003804070407700302

Coburn, C. E. (2006). Framing the problem of reading instruction: Using frame analysis to uncover the microprocesses of policy implementation. *American Educational Research Journal, 43*(3), 343–349. doi:10.3102/00028312043003343

Coburn, C. E., Hill, H. C., & Spillane, J. P. (2016). Alignment and accountability in policy design and implementation: The common core state standards and implementation research. *Educational Researcher, 45*(4), 243–251. doi:10.3102/0013189X16651080

Common Core State Standards Initiative. (2015a). *Understanding the common core state standards initiative*. Retrieved from http://commoncore.pearsoned.com/index.cfm?locator=PS11Ue

Common Core State Standards Initiative. (2015b). *About the standards*. National Governors Association. Retrieved from http://www.corestandards.org/about-the-standards/

Common Core State Standards Initiative. (2015c). *Development process*. National Governors Association. Retrieved from http://www.corestandards.org/about-the-standards/development-process/

Corbin, J. M., & Strauss, A. L. (2015). *Basics of qualitative research: Techniques and procedures for developing grounded theory* (4th ed.). Thousand Oaks, CA: Sage Publications.

Creswell, J. W. (2013). *Research design: Qualitative, quantitative, and mixed methods approaches* (4th ed.). Thousand Oaks, California: Sage Publications.

Croft, A., Coggshall, J. G., Dolan, M., Powers, E., & Killion, J. (2010). *Job-embedded professional development: What it is, who is responsible, and how to get it done well*. National Staff Development Council. Retrieved from http://www.gtlcenter.org/sites/default/files/docs/JEPD%20Issue%20Brief.pdf

Desimone, L. M. (2009). Improving impact studies of teachers' professional development: Toward better conceptualizations and measures. *Educational Researcher, 38*(3), 181–199. doi:10.3102/0013189X08331140

Durand, F. T., Lawson, H. A., Wilcox, K. C., & Schiller, K. S. (2016). The role of district office leaders in the adoption and implementation of the common core state standards in elementary schools. *Educational Administration Quarterly, 52*(1), 45–74. doi:10.1177/0013161X15615391

Firestone, W. A., Mangin, M. M., Martinez, M. C., & Polovsky, T. (2005). Leading coherent professional development: A comparison of three districts. *Educational Administration Quarterly, 41*(3), 413–448. doi:10.1177/0013161X0426960

Goals 2000 (1994): Educate America Act, Pub. L. 103–227, 108 Stat. 125, codified as amended in 20 U.S.C. (1994).

Goldstein, D. (2014). *The teacher wars: A history of America's most embattled profession*. New York, NY: Doubleday.

Gordon, S. P. (2004). *Professional development for school improvement: Empowering learning communities*. Boston, MA: Allyn & Bacon.

Greenleaf, C. L., Litman, C., Hanson, T. L., Rosen, R., Boscardin, C. K., Herman, J., & Jones, B. (2011). Integrating literacy and science in biology teaching and learning impacts of reading apprenticeship professional development. *American Educational Research Journal, 48*(3), 647–717. doi:10.3102/0002831210384839

Hakuta, K., Santos, M., & Fang, Z. (2013). Challenges and opportunities for language learning in the context of the CCSS and the NGSS. *Journal of Adolescent & Adult Literacy, 56*(6), 451–454. doi:10.1002/JAAL.164

Jagger, S. L., & Yore, L. D. (2012). Mind the gap: Looking for evidence-based practice of science literacy for all in science teaching journals. *Journal of Science Teacher Education, 23*(6), 559–577. doi:10.1007/s10972-012-9271-6

Johnson, C. C. (2013). Educational turbulence: The influence of macro and micro-policy on science education reform. *Journal of Science Teacher Education, 24*(4), 693–715. doi:10.1007/s10972-012-9333-9

Kaufman, J., Thompson, L., & Opfer, V. (2016) *Creating a coherent system to support instruction aligned with state standards: Promising practices of the Louisiana department of education*. Santa Monica, CA: Rand Corporation.

Kendall, J. (2011). *Understanding common core state standards*. Alexandria, VA: Association of Supervision and Curriculum Development.

Killion, J. (2013). Tapping technology's potential. *Journal of Staff Development, 34*(1), 10–18. Retrieved from https://learningforward.org/publications/jsd

Lee, O., Quinn, H., & Valdés, G. (2013). Science and language for English language learners in relation to next generation science standards and with implications for common core state standards for English language arts and mathematics. *Educational Researcher*, 1–11. doi:10.3102/0013189X13480524

Lewis, C., Perry, R., & Hurd, J. (2004). A deeper look at lesson study. *Educational Leadership, 61*(5), 18–22. Retrieved from http://www.ascd.org/publications/educational-leadership.aspx

Means, B., Toyama, Y., Murphy, R., Bakia, M., & Jones, K. (2009). *Evaluation of evidence-based practices in online learning: A meta-analysis and review of online learning studies*. Washington, DC: U.S. Department of Education, Office of Planning, Evaluation, and Policy Development.

National Research Council. (2012). *A framework for K–12 science education: Practices, crosscutting concepts, and core ideas*. Washington, DC: National Academies Press.

NGSS Lead States. (2013). *Next Generation Science Standards: For states, by states*. Washington, DC: National Academies Press.

Penuel, W., Fishman, B. J., Gallagher, L. P., Korbak, C., & Lopez-Prado, B. (2009). Is alignment enough? Investigating the effects of state policies and professional development on science curriculum implementation. *Science Education, 93*(4), 656–677. doi:10.1002/sce.20321

Pruitt, S. L. (2014). The next generation science standards: The features and challenges. *Journal of Science Teacher Education, 25*(2), 145–156. doi:10.1007/s10972-014-9385-0

Reiser, B. J. (2014). *Designing coherent storylines aligned with NGSS for the K–12 classroom*. Paper presented at the National Science Education Leadership Association Meeting. Boston, MA.

Sandoval, W. (2014). Conjecture mapping: An approach to systematic educational design research. *Journal of the Learning Sciences, 23*(1), 18–36. doi:10.1080/10508406.2013.778204

Severance, S., Penuel, W. R., Sumner, T., & Leary, H. (2016). Organizing for teacher agency in curricular co-design. *Journal of the Learning Sciences, 25*(4), 531–564. doi:10.1080/10508406.2016.1207541

Spencer, D., & Bouwma-Gearhart, J. (2014). Reading strategies for secondary science teachers. *Academic Exchange Quarterly, 18*(3). Retrieved from http://www.rapidintellect.com/AEQweb/

Surrette, T. N., & Johnson, C. C. (2015). Assessing the ability of an online environment to facilitate the critical features of teacher professional development. *School Science and Mathematics, 115*(6), 260–270. doi:10.1111/ssm.12132

Tong, F., Irby, B. J., Lara-Alecio, R., & Koch, J. (2014). Integrating literacy and science for English language learners: From learning-to-read to reading-to-learn. *Journal of Educational Research, 107*(5), 410–426. doi:10.1080/00220671.2013.833072

U.S. Congress. (2001). *No Child Left Behind Act of 2001. Public Law 107-110. 107th Congress.* Washington, DC: Government Printing Office. Retrieved from http://www.ed.gov/policy/elec/leg/esea02/107-110.pdf

Voogt, J., Laferrière, T., Breuleux, A., Itow, R. C., Hickey, D. T., & McKenney, S. (2015). Collaborative design as a form of professional development. *Instructional Science, 43*(2), 259–282. doi:10.1007/s11251-014-9340-7

Waring, S. M. (2016). Teaching with primary sources: Moving from professional development to a model of professional learning. In T. Petty, A. Good, & M. Putnam (Eds.), *Handbook of Research on Professional Development for Quality Teaching and Learning* (pp. 295–306). Hershey, PA: Information Science Reference.

Whitworth, B. A., Maeng, J. L., Wheeler, L. B., & Chiu, J. L. (2017). Investigating the role of a district science coordinator. *Journal of Research in Science Teaching, 54*(7), 914–936. doi:10.1002/tea.21391

Zepeda, S. J. (2012). *Professional development: What works.* New York, NY: Routledge.

Zepeda, S. J. (2015). *Job-embedded professional development: Support, collaboration, and learning in schools.* New York, NY: Routledge.

Chapter 5

Professional Development: Using Appreciative Inquiry to Understand the Perspectives of High School Mathematics Teachers

James M. Meneguzzo

SCENARIO

Ms. Haskins and Ms. Black are having a conversation about their teaching practice. As all good educators do, they often think about how they can improve their teaching practice to help improve their students' learning. Ms. Haskins has been teaching for 8 years and Ms. Black has been teaching for 15 years. They begin to talk about the professional development they have participated in during their years as teachers.

The discussion focuses on the types of professional development they need as high school math teachers to help them improve their instructional practices and have a more positive impact on their students' learning. Ms. Haskins and Ms. Black are dedicated to their own lifelong learning, engaged with their colleagues during collaborative planning periods, and dedicated to meeting the needs of their students.

KEY IDEAS IN THIS CHAPTER

- Understand what teachers need regarding professional development to support their instructional and classroom practices.
- Explore how using appreciative inquiry can help teachers become more involved with professional learning.

ABSTRACT

This chapter examines the perspectives of nine high school teachers of mathematics by (1) using appreciative inquiry as a means to identify their professional development needs and (2) exploring what the teachers identify as key factors to successful professional development to support their teaching practices.

INTRODUCTION

It is important that students be prepared to meet the demands of today's workforce as well as educational environments that extend beyond K–12. According to Chong and Kong (2012), "to prepare students with complex analytical skills to meet educational and work challenges of the 21st century, teachers must learn new ways of teaching that have a significant effect on student learning" (p. 263).

If the expectation for schools is to produce students who possess the higher-order thinking skills necessary to be successful in the 21st century, then school systems must provide teachers with the professional learning necessary for them to engage as lifelong learners who have higher-order thinking skills along with deep content knowledge (Darling-Hammond, Wei, Andree, Richardson, & Orphanos, 2009). One avenue for teacher learning is through professional development.

This chapter examines the perspectives of high school teachers of mathematics related to professional development. Appreciative inquiry research methods were used to examine what was "good" about professional development for teachers of high school mathematics. The foundational methods inherent in appreciative inquiry engage participants in the process of the "4-D phases"—discovery, dream, design, and destiny—to chart the positive attributes that lead teachers toward growth and development related to professional learning.

This chapter offers highlights of effective professional development in general and specifically in the area of mathematics, the methods involved in appreciative inquiry research, and the findings from a study of nine teachers of mathematics. A discussion of the findings from this study as well as implications for school leaders is offered.

OVERVIEW OF THE LITERATURE

With the current state of affairs regarding our students' mathematics scores, the need for effective professional development of mathematics teachers is important in today's educational environment. Providing professional growth opportunities for teachers is important if administrators expect them to provide their students with the best educational environment possible.

Gabriel, Day, and Allington (2011) recommended that to support their professional growth, teachers need purposeful and structured professional development opportunities, continuous support from other teachers and administrators, and the ability to provide input on the types of professional development opportunities offered individually and collectively within teams. Effective professional development generally and then specifically related to mathematics teachers is offered to frame this study.

Effective Professional Development

Darling-Hammond et al. (2009) suggested that effective professional development must include a focus on specific curriculum content and added that professional development needs to align with school and district initiatives as well as help support strong collaborative relationships among teachers. Core features of effective professional development programs must

- focus on specified content areas and instructional strategies (Darling-Hammond et al., 2009; Darling-Hammond, Hyler, & Gardner, 2017; Desimone, 2011);
- provide active learning opportunities with built-in follow-up that could include, for example, peer coaching, action research, informal and formal classroom observations, and sustained conversations about practice to guide ongoing efforts to grow as a professional (Zepeda, 2012, 2015);
- employ purposefully the processes, methods, and approaches that bring unity and coherence to efforts within and across schools and their systems (Leo & Coggshall, 2013; Zepeda, 2012, 2015); and
- honor the adult learner (Booth & Schwartz, 2012; Knowles, Swanson, & Holton, 2011).

Darling-Hammond and McLaughlin (2011) reported that the more teachers are actively involved in the learning process the more they gain from professional development.

Creating a collaborative learning environment is important for teachers because they have vast knowledge and experiences pertaining to their field that they value and want to share with colleagues. As teachers share their experiences, they learn from their colleagues as well as gain information that can be practical and useful in their classrooms. Teachers that are involved in interactive learning situations where they are able to discuss their teaching practices as well as problems dealing with classroom situations are better able to reflect, adapt, and grow as professionals (Darling-Hammond et al., 2017; Desimone, 2011).

Professional Development for Mathematics Teachers

Teaching math can be a difficult and complex process. It requires that teachers have a deep understanding of mathematical content as well as knowledge about how students develop through different grade levels (Daro, Mosher, & Corcoran, 2011). Teachers of mathematics need professional development that helps enhance their practice as well as their students' learning. The National Council of Teachers of Mathematics (2014) lists eight teaching practices that they consider essential in helping students gain a deeper understanding of mathematical content.

1. Establish mathematics goals to focus on learning.
2. Implement tasks that promote reasoning and problem solving.
3. Use and connect mathematical representations.
4. Facilitate meaningful mathematical discourse.
5. Pose purposeful questions.
6. Build procedural fluency from conceptual understanding.
7. Support productive struggle in learning mathematics.
8. Elicit and use evidence of student thinking. (p. 10)

Teachers of mathematics need to implement these types of specific mathematical teaching practices to help ensure they are (1) providing the type of instruction that supports students in their learning and (2) applying the principles of mathematics (Holmstrom, 2010).

CONTEXT OF THE STUDY

The participants in this study were nine math teachers from two different high schools within a school district located in a rural town geographically about 45 minutes from a major city. The district serves about 19,500 students with 18 elementary schools, five middle schools, three high schools, and two schools of choice. The school district serves a diverse population in both ethnicity and socioeconomic status. The high schools are representative of the school district in which they are located.

The two high schools chosen for this study were Asher High School and Nike High School (both pseudonyms). Asher High School served 1,964 students and Nike High School served 2,359 students at the time of the study. The ethnographic makeup of Nike High School was predominately African American while Asher High School was more similar to the district ethnographic makeup. The free and reduced lunch rate at Nike High School was 73.42% while at Asher High School it was 63.85%. The number of students that passed the Coordinate Algebra and Analytic Geometry/Mathematics II End of Course tests at Asher High School was about 7–10% higher on each test than at Nike High School.

The nine teachers that participated in the study ranged in years of teaching experience from three years to 27 years. The participants taught in each of the grade levels represented in the high schools, 9–12, and there was a wide range of courses taught, from ninth grade Algebra I to 12th grade pre-calculus. Of the nine participants, six were female, three were male, seven were African American, and two were white.

RESEARCH METHODS

Appreciative inquiry methods were used in this study. Appreciative inquiry is a philosophy that incorporates the "4-D process" for the purpose of engaging people at some level, within some type of organization, to help produce a positive and effective change (Cooperrider, Whitney, & Stavros, 2008). In using appreciative inquiry, the researcher assumes that within the organization there are things being done well and, therefore, positive change can be brought about by focusing on these strengths (Cooperrider et al., 2008).

Appreciative inquiry is used to build on strengths. A focus on the participants' positive experiences helps the participants feel a sense of commitment, confidence, and affirmation regarding the positive change that can take place (Clarke, Egan, Fletcher, & Ryan, 2006). In the 4-D process,

- *discovery* is the process of "appreciating and valuing" what is good about the organization;
- *dream* is the process of "envisioning" what a perfect organization would look like;
- *design* is the process of "co-constructing the future" to get the organization to look like what is envisioned in the dream process; and
- *destiny* is about "learning, empowering, and improvising to sustain the future." (Cooperrider et al., 2008, p. 5)

By using appreciative inquiry, the hope was to gain a better understanding of what teachers believe is effective professional development based on their experiences.

Appreciate inquiry allowed the researcher to focus teachers on what they already believed was good or effective regarding the professional development they had participated in and how these areas of strength could be used to help improve their future professional development to bring about positive changes in their teaching practices.

The nine teachers were each interviewed once, and the interviews ranged from 60 to 75 minutes long. The interviews were conducted in the privacy of the participant's classroom. The interviews were transcribed verbatim. The researcher listened to an audio recording of each interview while following its transcription to ensure accuracy as well as listen for inflection, pauses, and other verbal cues. During data analysis, codes were developed by using line-by-line coding that entailed "coding each fragment of the data" (Wertz et al., 2011, p. 172). The line-by-line coding helped the researcher find phrases or quotes that best expressed details about the research questions.

FINDINGS

The findings were organized by the order of the research questions. Presentation of the data in this way was important because of the use of the appreciative inquiry method and the 4-D model. Therefore, it made sense to analyze the data with respect to each question that represented each cycle of the model and to present the data in the same manner. The data are presented in the following manner based on the order of the research questions:

1. How do high school mathematics teachers describe their best professional development experiences? (Discovery)
2. How would high school mathematics teachers design professional development that would best supported their teacher practice? (Dream/Design)
3. How can high school mathematics teachers continuously engage themselves in professional development that will best support their teacher practice? (Destiny)

Discovery

In the discovery phase, participants should "appreciate and value" what is already good about professional development. "My best professional development would be one where I feel like I received enough information that I could immediately take it back to the class and use it a lot," stated Ms.

Bear. The best professional development experiences excited teachers because they felt they had learned something that they could implement in their classrooms. Ms. March explained it this way: "So, I think, those are the best ones where you come away from it feeling like I got some great ideas and I'm eager to go try them out now with my students."

The participants spoke about the importance of content, suggesting "the best content would be information that directly relates to my own subject and content" and is "geared toward the subject I teach at the level that I teach." For the participants, not only did the professional development sessions need to be about mathematics, but the sessions also needed to be very specific with regard to the math content areas. The participants wanted content to be transferable from theory into practice so they could take it back and use it in their classroom.

The participants noted that time for reflection was an important part of professional development—whether that reflection was with colleagues or self-reflection. Ms. March described the importance of having time to reflect with colleagues during a professional development experience. Ms. Bear shared the importance of having the opportunity to talk to other teachers who were "right there with you." The participants thought it equally important to have time to discuss with colleagues and have time by themselves to reflect on how the strategies learned would work in their classrooms.

Dream/Design

The dream phase is about envisioning the future, and the design phase is about co-constructing the future. With respect to high school mathematics professional development, this step examined how the teachers would design professional development sessions. The participants felt professional development sessions needed some type of hands-on learning where "we have to move, to touch, and to build," stated Ms. Bear. Ms. Black added that this meant "not only just getting information but also creating something tangible from what we are learning." Essentially, the participants felt strongly that professional development experiences needed to provide an opportunity for teachers to be able to develop something that they could take back and use in their classroom.

The participants believed it was important to include time for discussion during the professional development session. The discussion time would allow teachers to work together "so we can stop and ask how would this work for you in your classroom," said Mr. Johnson. Not only was it important for the teachers to have time to talk to each other about how what they were learning would work for them and their students, it was also important to allow time for the teachers to share any new ideas they had that might be helpful to their colleagues. Mr. Waters stated, "Allow us time to sit, discuss, think, and sketch out ideas with everybody else." The participants also wanted opportunities to work on ideas "in a small group setting to discuss and reflect" on what they learned and how this would be applicable in their classrooms.

The last item the participants discussed was making sure they felt supported once the professional development session ended. The participants needed to know that they had support in their classrooms while implementing what they learned during professional development opportunities. Ms. Byrd said the participants needed "some type of follow up from the professional development, including feedback on implementing ideas in the classroom." Ms. Byrd went on to add that getting support was not something that occurred often: "It's the follow-up piece that we usually don't get when we have professional development. You go one day and then, okay, go ahead and use it in your room."

Destiny

The destiny phase is about learning, empowering, and improvising to sustain the future (Cooperrider et al., 2008). This process was used to examine what teachers would do to help sustain their professional growth. It was interesting to note that the participants did not talk about formal professional development, such as attending professional development sessions; rather, they talked about informal professional development.

One way the participants believed they would continue to grow professionally was by looking for resources that would help their teaching practices. This could be done by reading publications from professional organizations or using different online resources including, for example, Facebook, Twitter, and Pinterest. Ms. Bear said, "What came to mind is some of the professional organizations like the NCTM [National Council of Teachers of Mathematics]. I get the weekly newsletter. I get the *Mathematics Journal* mailed to my home."

Ms. Bear also noted, "Facebook, they have some nice articles on there about education. There are a lot of professional groups being developed through Facebook, and they share different articles." Ms. Short said, "I'm always searching on the Internet or Pinterest for different ideas and ways to probe, come up with different ways to present difficult concepts."

The participants also talked about the importance of learning from their colleagues as a way to grow professionally. This learning did not need to occur in a formal, professional development setting. The participants discussed how this can occur in informal settings as well. Ms. Haskins stated, "I would like to sit in a couple of teachers' classes. I would like to see what makes it good so I can bring ideas back to my classroom." Ms. Short added,

"I think some of us need to step outside of our classroom to see what others are doing and what's worked for them" because "there's some other ways you can do some things that could be just as effective or even more effective."

It was interesting to note that the participants felt they could learn from experienced teachers as well as less-experienced teachers. "I definitely value the wisdom of veteran teachers," stated Mr. Johnson. "I think we more experienced teachers can learn from the new teachers who are coming out of college and saying now they're doing it this way," added Ms. Hoskins. The participants felt that they could learn and grow professionally from their colleagues, both veteran and new teachers, and this learning could occur informally through classroom visits and conversations.

Professional growth can occur through learning from colleagues as well as learning from one's own experiences. The participants discussed how they grow professionally from the experiences that occur in their classrooms. Mr. Wishbone discussed how he learns every day by just observing what goes on in his classroom. Mr. Waters added, "It's just being in the classroom and just watching what's happening, trying stuff out, going back to the drawing board and seeing what else might work." Learning from one's experiences requires critical reflection on feedback received. All the participants mentioned reflection as necessary.

DISCUSSION OF FINDINGS

The key factors that high school mathematics teachers feel they need for effective professional development are examined, including relevance, content specificity, modeling, reflection, and feedback.

Relevance

The research suggests that adults learn best when they are self-directed; when new knowledge is built on their pre-existing knowledge; when learning is relevant to their life experiences, needs, and goals; and when the theoretical knowledge is easily transferable to a practical context (Knowles et al., 2011). We know that adults seek learning experiences that provide them with knowledge and skills that are applicable to their real-world experiences (Zepeda, 2012).

The participants in the study, based on the data, seemed to agree that the best or most effective professional development experiences were those that provided them with something that was relevant to them with respect to their classroom practice. While professional development experience needs to provide teachers with ideas, strategies, or some kind of product, it also needs to add to their existing knowledge base.

Content Specificity

The participants discussed how important it was that whatever they were learning in professional development be applicable to the content they were teaching at the time. Ms. May stated, "I think the best content would be information that directly relates to my own subject and content." Mr. Johnson and Ms. Sand added, respectively, "First, it is super specific to the content of my classroom" and "there were some specific examples geared to math . . . specifically how I can use it in my high school math class."

Professional development for math teachers, while having many of the same characteristics of what makes professional development effective for teachers across content areas, needs to focus specifically on instructional strategies that will support students' learning of mathematics (Holmstrom, 2010). Ms. Brown said, "I attended professional development about AP calculus, and I was like 'Wow!' because I didn't even know this was out there. . . . They gave me all kinds of resources and ways and projects and everything and that was good for me." When Ms. Short was asked what made a particular professional development experience she was discussing beneficial, she remarked that "it was geared toward the subject I teach at the [grade] level that I teach."

The participants also discussed how important it was that the ideas, strategies, and products discussed during professional development be easily implemented back in the classroom. Ms. May stated, "I feel like it has been effective information if we can implement it in the class. I think it has to be something that can practically be implemented," and Ms. Bear added, "It was easy to set up and did not take much for the students to understand what they had to do."

The participants also discussed how creating something in professional development could help implement what is being learned in the classroom. For Ms. Sand, the ideal professional development provided the opportunity to create a finished product that was ready to use "tomorrow in the classroom."

Modeling

The participants discussed the importance of seeing how an idea, strategy, or product discussed in professional development worked in the classroom. Ms. Sand discussed the importance of seeing how it would work with respect to the content that she was teaching, and she added emphatically, "Show me how that works in a high school math setting. We actually did it right there in the training, and that's when I thought, 'Oh, I could use this.'"

Reflection

The participants discussed the importance of having an opportunity to reflect. Reflection provides an opportunity for math teachers to think critically about what they have learned during professional development and how this can benefit their classroom practices. Reflection can also be used to think objectively about the implementation of what was learned or created in professional development. Ms. Short added, "Just really a self-reflection in terms of why didn't it work; is it the activity itself, is it just the classroom atmosphere?" Reflecting with colleagues can be beneficial during professional development, and Ms. Haskins said the best professional development occurs when "I can get feedback from colleagues before taking a strategy back to the classroom."

An opportunity for teachers to discuss and collaborate with their colleagues during professional development was very important, and this emerged during the dream/design phase. It is important for adults to have an opportunity to discuss and collaborate with other adults during learning experiences. Professional development experiences need to provide opportunities for teachers to discuss and to collaborate with their colleagues about what they are learning in professional development.

The participants noted the importance of teacher discussion and collaboration. Ms. March stated, "I think it is probably best that the facilitator starts out providing information and then shifts to letting the teachers discuss or explore how that is going to work." Ms. Haskins added, "Then we'll have time to talk and to get suggestions on what to do."

Discussion and collaboration provide teachers with an opportunity to talk about a learning experience and to share ideas with each other. This allows them to discuss how "this or that" will help them in the classroom or what could be done to help make these ideas work in the classroom.

Feedback

According to the participants, feedback would be an important component of any professional development experience they would design. According to Ms. Hoskins, "So I think feedback is important and that it occurs right afterwards instead of waiting up to the end." Providing immediate feedback gives teachers the support they need to better transfer to their classroom what they have learned during their professional development experience. It is important that teachers receive feedback regarding their professional development experience.

Teachers need to be able to share what has worked and what has not worked with respect to implementing what they have learned. This feedback provides teachers with support in the transfer of the professional development experience to their classroom. Support is important and needs to be continuous so that professional development is not just a one-time thing but also something that occurs throughout the year.

IMPLICATIONS FOR SCHOOL LEADERS

There are a few implications that can be derived from this study. For the field of practice, the following ideas are offered to school and system leaders.

Ask teachers what they want from professional learning. Teachers are more than willing to speak about their learning needs. It is important that teachers have input into the type of professional development experiences they have. Based on this study's findings, the participants knew what professional development experiences they needed to benefit them. Therefore, it is important for district and school administrators to listen to teachers to find out what they need to help them grow professionally. One participant said it best: "Just ask us."

Provide time and opportunity for professional development. With the provision of time and opportunity during the day, professional learning becomes more job-embedded. By allowing teacher voice and input, there may be a greater chance that teachers will engage in the type of learning that leads to changes in their practices (Bass, 2012; Jurrow, 2009). If professional development is to be effective and have a positive influence on classroom practice, teachers must have input as to the type of professional development they participate in (Darling-Hammond & McLaughlin, 2011), and they must also be willing to invest the time and energy needed on behalf of their own learning (Zepeda, 2015).

Based on the findings of this study, another recommendation is that teachers be given time and opportunity for professional development to occur during periods of the day. The participants believed that professional development offered during planning or after school was an "add-on" to an already full day of working with children. For the teachers in this study, professional development could be an intrusion especially if it was not relevant to them.

School and district administrators need to understand this so that they can plan professional learning days for the school calendar. The findings suggested that teachers feel it was more important to learn from their colleagues, and administrators need to seek ways to provide teachers with opportunities to observe lessons as well as time for discussion and reflection after the observations.

Provide support for teachers "after" professional development to make learning a continuous process. Based on the findings of this study, teachers need support so that professional development is an ongoing process. Professional development often consists only of the teacher's attending a session and then being abandoned to figure "things out" about how to take what was learned in the session and put it into practice. Teachers need support in taking what was learned during the professional development experience and putting it into practice in their classroom. This support could include providing teachers with time to plan, with observational feedback, or with an opportunity to observe a colleague's use of the strategy.

SUMMARY

The findings of this study suggest that teachers have very basic needs related to professional development. Teachers need and want to be able to give input as to the type of professional development they participate in. They need and want opportunities to observe, discuss, and reflect with colleagues, and they need continuous support from the administration. The findings of this study suggest that teachers want and need opportunities to collaborate with colleagues to help them to grow professionally.

Discussion Questions
1. How do your district and school leaders allow teachers more input regarding the professional development they participate in?
2. How do your district and school leaders provide teachers with the support they need to participate in the kind of professional development they feel best influences their practices and student learning?
3. How can your district and school leaders provide more opportunities for teachers to participate in effective job-embedded professional learning experiences such as peer coaching?

SUGGESTED READINGS

Gersten, R., Taylor, M. J., Keys, T. D., Rolfhus, E., & Newman-Gonchar, R. (2014). Summary of research on the effectiveness of math professional development approaches. Regional Educational Laboratory Southeast. REL 2014-010. Retrieved from http://rel-se.fcrr.org

Hargreaves, A. (2014). Foreword: Six sources of change in professional development. In L. E. Martin, S. Kragler, D. J. Quatroche, & K. L. Bauserman (Eds.), *Handbook of professional development in education: Successful models and practices, PreK–12* (pp. x–xix). New York, NY: Guilford.

REFERENCES

Bass, C. (2012). Learning theories & their application to science instruction for adults. *American Biology Teacher, 74*(6), 387–390. doi:10.1525/abt.2012.74.6.6

Booth, M., & Schwartz, H. L. (2012). We're all adults here: Clarifying and maintaining boundaries with adult learners. *New Directions for Teaching & Learning, 2012*(131), 43–55. doi:10.1002/tl.20026

Chong, W. H., & Kong, C. A. (2012). Teacher collaborative learning and teacher self-efficacy: The case of lesson study. *Journal of Experimental Education, 80*(3), 263–283. doi:10.1080/00220973.2012.10806591

Clarke, H., Egan, B., Fletcher, L., & Ryan, C. (2006). Creating case studies of practice through appreciative inquiry. *Educational Action Research, 14*(3), 407–422. doi:10.1080/09650790600847776

Cooperrider, D. L., Whitney, D., & Stavros, J. M. (2008). *Appreciative inquiry handbook for leaders of change* (2nd ed.). Brunswick, OH: Crown Custom Publishing.

Darling-Hammond, L., Hyler, M. E., & Gardner, M. (2017). Effective teacher professional development. Palo Alto, CA: Learning Policy Institute. Retrieved from https://learningpolicyinstitute.org/product/effective-teacher-professional-development-brief

Darling-Hammond, L., & McLaughlin, M. W. (2011). Policies that support professional development in an era of reform. *Phi Delta Kappan, 92*(6), 81–92. doi:10.1177/003172171109200622

Darling-Hammond, L., Wei, R. C., Andree, A., Richardson, N., & Orphanos, S. (2009). *A status report on teacher development in the United States and abroad.* Retrieved from http://learningforward.org/docs/pdf/nsdcstudytechnicalreport2009.pdf?sfvrsn=0

Daro, P. F., Mosher, F. A., & Corcoran, T. (2011). *Learning trajectories in mathematics: A foundation for standards, curriculum, assessment, and instruction.* Philadelphia, PA: Consortium for Policy Research in Education.

Desimone, L. M. (2011). A primer on effective professional development. *Phi Delta Kappan, 92*(6), 68–71. doi:10.1177/003172171109200616

Gabriel, R., Day, J. P., & Allington, R. (2011). Exemplary teacher voices on their own development. *Phi Delta Kappan, 92*(8), 37–41. doi:10.1177/003172171109200808

Holmstrom, A. (2010). District finds the right equation to improve math instruction. *Journal of Staff Development, 31*(6), 58–62. Retrieved from http://www.nsdc.org/news/jsd/index.cfm

Jurrow, A. S. (2009). Cultivating self in the context of transformative professional development. *Journal of Teacher Education, 60*(3), 277–290. doi:10.1177/0022487109336895

Knowles, M. S., Swanson, R. A., & Holton, E. F. (2011). *Adult learner: The definitive classic in adult education and human resource development* (7th ed.). New York, NY: Routledge.

Leo, S. F., & Coggshall, J. G. (2013). Creating coherence: Common Core State Standards, teacher evaluation, and professional learning. Washington, DC: Center on Great Teachers and Leaders, American Institutes for Research. Retrieved from http://www.gtlcenter.org/sites/default/files/CreatingCoherence.pdf

National Council of Teachers of Mathematics. (2014). *Principles to actions: Ensuring mathematical success for all.* Retrieved from http://www.nctm.org/

Wertz, F. J., Charmaz, K., McMullen, L. M., Josselson, R., Anderson, R., & McSpadden, E. (2011). *Five ways of doing qualitative analysis: Phenomenological psychology, grounded theory, discourse analysis, narrative research, and intuitive inquiry.* New York, NY: Guilford Press.

Zepeda, S. J. (2012). *Professional development: What works* (2nd ed.). New York, NY: Routledge.

Zepeda, S. J. (2015). *Job-embedded professional development: Support, collaboration, and learning in schools.* New York, NY: Routledge.

Chapter 6

Lessons Learned About Job-Embedded Learning

Sally J. Zepeda

KEY IDEAS IN THIS CHAPTER

- Teacher agency and professional learning
- Processes of professional learning
- Professional learning cultures
- Lessons for school leaders

In each chapter of this book, numerous lessons about the nature of job-embedded professional learning have been identified. The authors identify and discuss the types of support that school leaders need to ensure are available for teachers to grow and to develop.

The authors have illuminated best practices in professional learning and the structures that support teacher development. They reported interesting findings about the potential of certain structural supports that give teachers opportunities to learn from the work of teaching and from working with their colleagues. In some instances, the authors magnify why some practices related to professional learning did not work. By doing so, the authors deepen our understanding and provide insights for school leaders to consider.

Overall, this chapter examines the findings and our need to understand teacher agency related to professional learning. In addition, this chapter focuses our attention on the processes associated with professional learning, professional learning cultures, and the lessons school leaders need to consider related to their work with teachers.

TEACHER AGENCY AND PROFESSIONAL LEARNING

The construct of human agency is not a new one (Bandura, 2006), but there is a renewed interest focusing on teacher agency especially centering on professional learning (Calvert, 2016; Philpott & Oates, 2016; Zepeda, 2015). This focus is important. Teacher agency aligns with what we know about job-embedded professional learning (Buxton, Allexsaht-Snider, Kayumova, Aghasaleh, Choi, & Cohen, 2015; Calvert, 2016; Noonan, 2016; Zepeda, 2015). Calvert (2016) notes that teacher agency is "the capacity of teachers to act purposefully and constructively to direct their professional growth and contribute to the growth of their colleagues" (p. 4).

Characteristics of agency

Noonan (2016) states that teachers exert agency when they have choices and make decisions about their professional learning. Choice and voice situates the teacher as an active participant prior to, during, and after professional learning. Across the chapters, key characteristics related to teacher agency can be drawn from the rich portrayals of teachers who benefit from professional learning when it

1. Affirms that teachers are more than capable of making decisions about what they need and want from professional learning and can actively plan and assess the impact of their learning. When necessary, teachers can reset the direction of their learning.
2. Places value on collaboration with colleagues. Collaborating with colleagues about practice promotes shared opportunities for teachers to learn from each other.
3. Promotes learning that is enhanced with support structures such as reflection, peer coaching, etc.
4. Champions learning that is personalized and differentiated based on the developmental needs of teachers—across the career continuum.

These four areas are characteristic of teacher agency and are examined in relation to the findings presented by the chapter authors.

Two perspectives are offered before proceeding with a discussion of teacher agency. First, these areas often intersect with one another, and in many ways, these characteristics are multidimensional. For example, teachers who exert agency are decision-makers, and their needs as adult learners are more than likely met through active engagement in not only their own learning but also the learning that occurs collaboratively with colleagues.

Second, not every study illustrated that teachers held agency for their learning or that job-embedded learning was the norm where teachers actively learned from their work. For example, the teachers in Michael P. Cassidy's study (Chapter 4) "endured" professional learning that was mandated by external reform, the implementation of the Common Core State Standards. The situation for these teachers was confounded as there were two different playbooks. The district instructional coach presented professional learning on Next Generation Science Standards; however, the system and its curricular materials focused on the Common Core State Standards. The principal did not intervene. Coherence was lacking.

In a similar vein, the high school teachers of mathematics in James M. Meneguzzo's study (Chapter 5) wanted to be decision-makers in their professional learning, but they were rarely afforded the opportunity to do so. Through appreciative inquiry methods, we learn about the best professional learning these teachers had and why these opportunities were "the best." The findings of this study can support school leaders and others that frame professional learning according to a model of what occurs before, during, and after professional development is delivered.

Affirms the Teacher as Decision-Maker

For the teachers in Jen Cole's study (Chapter 3), decision-making was at the heart of learning. The teachers took control of what they learned, how they learned it, and what to do with what they had learned. For these teachers, collaboration became shared accountability and fostered taking responsibility for their learning and the learning of their colleagues, ensuring that there was trickle-down to the classroom—the students. Cole's study is an important one because it illustrates how goal setting can link instructional supervision, teacher evaluation, and professional learning in a seamless process to support teacher growth and development.

Participants were able to work with a cross-section of teachers not only from within their teams but also from other grade levels and teams based on other goals. The goals were related to the areas that the teachers self-identified or identified with the support of the principal. Although the goals were related to the prior year's evaluation and the current year's professional goals for development, the program was not an administrative one.

The goal groups were organized by the instructional coach, and the teachers who self-selected into the topically related goal groups "owned" the workings of the groups. There was an organizing structure to the goal groups, but the teachers governed their own learning. Goal group members set the parameters of when they would meet and how they would share information. Using a Google platform, many of the teachers collaborated online and over the weekends beyond the regularly scheduled meeting times after school and during planning periods.

In Chapter 5, James M. Meneguzzo used the appreciative inquiry method to get high school mathematics teachers to think about their own professional learning. During interviews, the nine high school mathematics teachers were first asked simply, "What's right and good about professional learning?" Next, the teachers were asked to identify their professional development needs and to identify and discuss the key processes that would enable them to grow as teachers. The processes included, for example, hands-on experiences and feedback on the implementation of new content knowledge.

Interview data from Meneguzzo's study illustrated that the teachers were decisive and did not hesitate to elaborate on what they needed from professional learning. In sum, the teachers wanted professional learning that allowed them to reflect and engage in collaborative discussions with peers. They wanted professional learning opportunities that were geared toward their specific content areas in mathematics.

The teachers in Meneguzzo's study said that generalized forms of professional learning were not specific enough to support development of content knowledge or the pedagogical methods needed to address a refinement of instruction in mathematics. From Meneguzzo's study, we learned that all we have to do is just ask teachers—they are more than capable of identifying what they need and want to grow as professionals.

Values Collaboration

In Chapter 2, Brandi Wade Worsham reports that collaboration during weekly formal content meetings helped teachers to combat feelings of isolation because they were able to encourage each other to take risks by trying new instructional strategies. Informally, collaboration was a staple for these teachers as they checked in with each other during class changes, lunch, or any other opportune time during the day.

The big take-away from Worsham's study is that it was through collaboration that teachers were able to make sense of what they were learning from the work of teaching. Moreover, collaboration helped the teachers to refocus on refining their teaching practices and to make sense of the changes that were occurring because of the ongoing support they were able to offer each other.

Jen Cole (Chapter 3) reports that through collaboration teachers became more intrinsically motivated to work toward achieving individual and group goals and that teachers were more focused on sustained discussions especially related to instruction. It was through the collaborative cultures within the group structures that relationships were built. Moreover, Cole found that collaboration had a trickle-down effect that shaped and reshaped the overall school culture to one of a learning culture for teachers.

In a similar vein, James M. Meneguzzo (Chapter 5) reported that the nine high school mathematics teachers overwhelmingly believed that professional learning that did not include collaborative processes such as discussion, feedback, and follow-up was ineffective. Collaboration is important, and Riveros, Newton, and Burgess (2012) suggest that "school-based peer collaboration is one among many possible ways in which teachers can learn about their profession, exercise their agency in school settings, and contribute to the educational success of their students" (p. 204).

Includes Support Structures

In all the chapters of this book, the authors describe and explain the various support structures involved in job-embedded learning for adults. It was through targeted conversations, follow-up support by peers and school leaders, collaboration during team meetings, and coaching opportunities that teachers learned from their practices.

Meneguzzo's research (Chapter 5) presents a detailed examination of the structures that teachers need and want following formal and informal professional learning opportunities. For these teachers, the support structures were in many ways more important than the formal professional learning in that they could engage with their colleagues, drawing on "live" examples from their classroom practices. On the other hand, the worst type of follow-up occurred for the teachers in Cassidy's study (Chapter 4) because it involved incessant meetings that left teachers feeling "meeting'd out."

Champions Personalized Learning

Personalization is foundational to support teachers as they identify gaps in their skills, work on strategies and content to eliminate gaps, and continually refine their practices—while owning their learning. Personalization can be achieved through a variety of ways, most notably in the processes involved with embedding learning in the work day.

THE PROCESSES OF PROFESSIONAL LEARNING

Reading these chapters, we find that teachers want professional learning that is hands-on, sustained, relevant to their work with students, and has immediate application—the next day in their classrooms. They also want variety in the "form" of job-embedded opportunities—action research, collaborative classroom observations with follow-up conversations, and studying student work, for example. They learn alongside others, including instructional coaches and team and grade-level members. Jen Cole (Chapter 3) describes a school-wide program for all teachers: collaborative goal groups.

Overall, teachers want structures that include uninterrupted time during the day to collaborate; dedicated meeting spaces; follow-up supports that include, for example, feedback from peers on classroom practices; and ongoing conversations with not only peers but also with school leaders. Brandi Wade Worsham (Chapter 2) reminds us that reflection, collaboration, and application are key features (e.g., process) of effective professional learning.

Processes that provide content focus, active learning, and collective participation serve as reminders of how the features of job-embedded learning, grounded in practice and daily reflection, promote collegiality, facilitate application and adaptation, and adhere to the principles of adult learning. Worsham concludes that all of these processes help teachers construct new knowledge and skills—and moreover, this is how teachers make sense of their learning.

Michael P. Cassidy (Chapter 4) offers a poignant account of what happens when professional learning activities lack coherence between standards and when the instructional practices championed during professional learning are counter to the methods suggested by standards. Cassidy amplifies in his discussion what happens when professional learning lacks coherence. Cassidy also magnifies the divide between the building and the central office level leaders. This divide created havoc for teachers who had to sift through mixed messages, endure excessive meetings, and experience "little to no" follow-through.

Job-Embedded Learning

Although examined in Chapter 1 and in each of the following chapters, a short refresher on job-embedded learning is important. Job-embedded learning is a multifaceted construct. The processes and attributes of job-embedded learning work in tandem to support teachers as they work with students in their classrooms. Zepeda (2015) reports that job-embedded learning

- *enhances reflection* through inquiry and sustained conversations with others;
- *promotes collegiality* through work environments that flatten traditional hierarchies and eliminate structural barriers that prevent teachers from working with one another;

- *combats isolation* through purposeful structures that support teachers interacting with one another—time is reconfigured so that teachers can collaborate, co-plan, and learn on a nearly daily basis;
- *makes learning more relevant to each teacher* because professional development is a part of the teacher's daily practice and tailored to the teacher's specific learning needs;
- *increases transfer of newly learned* skills because when professional learning is embedded in the workday, learning *is* practice (teachers implement new techniques as they acquire them, and through sustained coaching and other forms of follow-up, transfer is usually assured); and
- *supports the ongoing refinement of practice* through sustained encouragement to make adjustments to what is learned through such efforts.

Job-embedded learning cannot emerge or be sustained in a culture that does not support these purposes and intents.

PROFESSIONAL LEARNING CULTURES

In a learning culture, teachers are engaged in the collaborative effort of learning. In a learning culture, teachers are committed to sharing their expertise and their experiences with their colleagues. Leaders who champion job-embedded learning can only do so effectively in a culture that supports teachers and their efforts to learn from the very work and interactions they have with students in their classrooms and during the day with their peers.

Building and maintaining a strong culture of professional learning inside schools takes work and time. At the forefront of such a culture is a foundation of trust. Teachers need and want to be "trusted to take risks" (Hauserman & Stick, 2013, p. 196). According to Tschannen-Moran (2014), "principals and teachers who trust each other can better work together in the service of solving the challenging problems of schooling. These leaders create a bond that helps to inspire teachers to move to a higher level of effort and achievement" (p. 13). Leaders need to engage teachers in authentic ways to take ownership and direct their own learning needs while simultaneously creating the conditions where teachers can collaborate. In a culture of trust, job-embedded learning is "a continuous thread that can be found throughout the culture of the school" (Zepeda, 2012, p. 125).

MacDonald (2013), however, offers a caveat for school leaders related to a veneer of trust and collaboration when leaders need to scan the environment looking out for the "possibility of a 'culture of alone together,' where people are teamed together but act alone. They are guarded in what they share and with whom, seeing collaboration as only necessary for people who need help and preferring to work in isolation" (p. 42).

LESSONS FOR SCHOOL LEADERS

Numerous lessons for school leaders emerged from the works of the authors, and each chapter ends with a section titled "Implications for School Leaders." The implications within each chapter are based logically on the findings of the study. Embedded within these implications are suggestions for school leaders to consider when leading professional learning.

First, for professional learning efforts to gain traction, teachers need supportive building leaders who will champion and advocate for them as they develop in the journey of learning to teach. Providing professional learning is more than an obligation to serve as a check-off for district accountability systems. Muijs et al. (2014, p. 249) remind us that "everyone who has a place in the chain of influence from policy to practice" must be present and attentive to ensure professional learning for teachers.

Second, the principal is the lead learner of the school (Zepeda, Parylo, & Klar, 2017) whose influence is second only to teachers in moving the needle toward student achievement (Hallinger, 2011). With the complexities associated with teaching and the never-ending metrics by which teachers are evaluated, they deserve our very best efforts to help them grow as professionals.

In no particular order, the lessons learned are presented for consideration. School and system leaders should examine how these notions can be incorporated as part of an overall strategy to ensure teachers continue to grow in the work they do to teach. The context of the school, the history of professional learning at the school, and the ways in which teachers have interacted in the past will dictate how these lessons can be translated into viable practices that are responsive to the needs of the building. Remember, *context is everything.*

Leaders need to create an environment where teachers are allowed to be responsible for their own professional learning, with well-placed supports in place. School leaders are responsible for the professional learning opportunities that occur in their schools, and much of what happens in schools is based on the culture that principals shape and nurture. As a leader, it makes sense to understand school culture as it relates to professional learning. As a starting point, begin by asking, What is the professional learning culture in this school? Here are some questions to guide the assessment.

1. Do teachers observe one another and give constructive feedback on what is observed?
2. Do teachers engage on a regular basis in collaborative planning? Co-teaching?
3. Do teachers participate in book studies? Action research? Lesson Study? Other activities that support job-embedded learning?
4. Do teachers set yearly professional learning goals? If so, what mechanism is in place to work with teachers to achieve these goals? Are teachers who have common professional learning goals paired to serve as support for each other? What happens when a teacher meets his or her learning goals?
5. Are there mentoring programs, peer coaching programs, and other types of support programs in place? If so, how populated are these programs, who works with the teachers involved in these programs, and have the outcomes of such programs been assessed to determine overall effectiveness related to the goals that led to their development?

The answers to these questions and more will help the leader assess not only the professional learning culture but also the level of involvement of teachers—and to what extent teachers have a voice and choice in the types of learning they engage.

Responses to the next two questions should also be examined.

1. Depending on the school culture and the history of professional learning in the building, do teachers understand what job-embedded leaning is?
2. Depending on the school culture and the history of professional learning in the building, what would teachers need to engage in job-embedded learning?

School leaders who champion teacher development make job-embedded learning public practice to engender a culture of learning and to create an ethos of participative involvement hopefully leading to and strengthening learning among teachers. Although leaders cannot abdicate their responsibility for providing opportunities and resources for teachers to engage in professional learning, they should invite teachers to be major players in their own learning.

We learned a simple but valuable lesson from James M. Meneguzzo (Chapter 5): "Just ask teachers" to identify their high-beam experiences with professional learning. Through careful listening to teachers' points of view about professional learning, school leaders will be able to act on what teachers need from professional learning. To listen and not to act means the school leader has not heard the messages. School leaders can empower and support agency by involving (1) teachers in planning for professional learning; (2) teacher leaders such as department chairs, grade level leaders, or any other teacher who wants to step up to the plate in the design of programs that fit the needs of the school, its school improvement plans and goals, and the particular needs of teachers; and (3) teachers in leading professional learning. Moreover, school leaders need to show that professional learning is important and that they are themselves lifelong learners.

Leaders need to consider teacher identity and motivation when designing and implementing job-embedded learning experiences. Attending to teacher identity and motivation may increase the likelihood that teachers will find professional learning experiences meaningful and valuable.

The construct of teacher identity is important to consider. McGriff (2015) offers a series of theoretical perspectives that can help us understand why teacher identity is important to consider related to professional learning. McGriff summarizes from her own work and the work of others that the development of teacher identity shares common core features:

- identity is predicated upon human interactions;
- identity is predicated upon interpretations of lived experiences;
- identity is a dynamic entity that develops continually over time; and
- identity incorporates aspects of an individual's interactions in a range of settings. (p. 83)

McGriff (2015) indicates that teacher identity "is inherently connected to participation in social practices" (p. 83), and Beijaard, Verloop, and Vermunt (2000) posit that "teachers' perceptions of their own professional identity affect their efficacy and professional development as well as their ability and willingness to cope with educational change and to implement innovations in their own teaching practice" (p. 750).

How a teacher's identity evolves over time is impossible to predict; however, beliefs and attitudes about professional learning and teacher identity can be shaped over time by the types of professional learning offered; the timing of professional learning via key markers in a teacher's career; and the ways in which learning with colleagues is approached.

In many ways, teachers need to be socialized as learners through and by professional development at the onset of their careers (1) to see the value of constantly learning with students and colleagues, and (2) to learn that the often thorny issues of practice can be approached in a fault-free environment with colleagues. Moreover, professional learning must continue as teachers move throughout their careers because needs change over time.

As a leader, it is imperative to know your teachers. What experiences do teachers bring with them to the school? What has shaped their beliefs and attitudes regarding professional learning? Brandi Wade Worsham (Chapter 2) suggests that school leaders consider the use of personality, learning style, or motivational surveys to learn more about the beliefs, understandings, and interests of their faculty prior to developing and implementing professional learning opportunities. Learning more about the background and experiences that have shaped teachers can lead to more personalized and differentiated learning experiences.

In line with the findings of James M. Meneguzzo's study (Chapter 5), school leaders need to engage teachers in conversations about their professional learning. From these conversations, understanding of the teacher's point-of-view becomes more clear and can guide professional learning as a communal practice, as was also discussed by Jen Cole (Chapter 3) in her examination of goal groups and how the teachers enacted their professional learning.

Leaders need to find time in the day for teachers to learn from one another and then they need to become vigilant about protecting this time. Lack of time is the bane of professional job-embedded learning. Teachers need time to meet and discuss teaching techniques, engage in data analysis centering on student work and performance, and provide assistance and reassurance while learning from practice and from peers vis-à-vis what they do in their classrooms and why it is important.

The perennial tension for school leaders is there is no magic bullet for finding time in the day for job-embedded learning. However, through some creative strategies, school leaders will be in a position to think through and perhaps reconfigure time for teachers during the day to engage in purposeful job-embedded learning. The following suggestions are offered as a starting point for school leaders:

1. Examine current ways in which teachers' time is organized. For example, do teachers have planning periods? Every day? If teachers have planning periods every day, work with teachers to dedicate time during these meetings for collaborative learning.
2. Include processes such as peer coaching where teachers visit each other's classrooms—for example, invest in substitute teachers so that teachers can be released for a period after a classroom observation. This time is an investment in promoting collaboration, reflection, and a learning culture.
3. Examine the development of school-wide initiatives such as book studies and action research.
4. Reconfigure traditional faculty meetings so a majority of the time is spent on professional learning. Involve teachers in the design and development of this idea.

Of course, collective bargaining agreements, policies related to teacher time (e.g., number of prep periods, duty periods), and other system-agreements must be examined to ensure that policies and procedures are not in jeopardy when massaging schedules to find time in the day.

Leaders must have a clear understanding of established content and performance standards across subject areas (e.g., mathematics, science, English) and grade levels. With these understandings and familiarity, school leaders must provide opportunities for professional learning that targets meeting and exceeding these standards related to content, instructional practices, and assessment strategies that align to meeting the needs of all students. Equally important are provisions to support teachers in the content-specific knowledge of the subjects and grade levels they teach. Work with instructional coaches to lead teachers in job-embedded learning activities with individual and teams of teachers. If your coaches have received the professional learning they need to enact their work, then they will be able to

- model, demonstrate, and co-teach with teachers;
- conduct targeted classroom observations with the standards in mind, engage in conversations about what they observe in targeted post-observation conferences, and provide follow-up assistance when necessary;
- lead teams of teachers in discussing the strengths of classroom practices, etc.; and
- work with teachers to analyze exemplars of student work samples, pre- and post-test data, and other artifacts that capture instruction and student competency.

School leaders need to monitor implementation and provide follow-up professional learning opportunities. In other words, school leaders do not have to be intimately knowledgeable about the standards, but they need to know enough to work with others such as instructional coaches, department chairs, and grade level-leaders so they can lead the work with teachers.

The reader is encouraged to return to the chapters to examine the specific insights that the authors offer for school leaders to consider. From the findings of these studies, new conversations need to emerge between teachers and leaders to frame professional learning that can make a difference in the lives of teachers as they learn from their work with students and their colleagues. When job-embedded learning is championed, both teachers and students will reap the benefits of these efforts.

SUGGESTED READINGS

Drago-Severson, E., Roy, P., & von Frank, V. (2015). *Reach the highest standard in professional learning: Learning designs.* Thousand Oaks, CA: Corwin.
Fullan, M., Quinn, J., & Adam, E. (2016). *The taking action guide to building coherence in schools, districts, and systems.* Thousand Oaks, CA: Corwin.
Tschannen-Moran, M. (2014). *Trust matters: Leadership for successful schools* (2nd ed.). San Francisco, CA: Jossey-Bass.

REFERENCES

Bandura, A. (2006). Toward a psychology of human agency: Perspectives on psychological science. *Association for Psychological Science, 1*(2), 164–180. doi:10.2307/40212163

Beijaard, D., Verloop, N., & Vermunt, J. D. (2000). Teachers' perceptions of professional identity: An exploratory study from a personal knowledge perspective. *Teaching and Teacher Education, 16*(7), 749–764. https://doi.org/10.1016/S0742-051X(00)00023-8

Buxton, C. A., Allexsaht-Snider, M., Kayumova, S., Aghasaleh, R., Choi, Y., & Cohen, A. (2015). Teacher agency and professional learning: Rethinking fidelity of implementation as multiplicities of enactment. *Journal of Research in Science Teaching, 52*(4), 489–502. doi:10.1002/tea.21223

Calvert, L. (2016). *Moving from compliance to agency: What teachers need to make professional learning work.* Oxford, OH: Learning Forward. Retrieved from https://learningforward.org/publications/teacher-agency

Hallinger, P. (2011). Leadership for learning: Lessons from 40 years of empirical research. *Journal of Educational Administration, 49*(2), 125–142. doi:10.1108/09578231111116699

Hauserman, C. P., & Stick, S. L. (2013). The leadership teachers want from principals: Transformational. *Canadian Journal of Education, 36*(3), 184–203. Retrieved from https://cje-rce.ca/

MacDonald, E. B. (2013). Turn obstacles into opportunities: Team leaders use a skillful approach to move past barriers to learning. *Journal of Staff Development, 34*(6), 38–49. Retrieved from http://learningforward.org/

McGriff, M. (2015). Teacher identity and EL-focused professional learning in a suburban middle school. *Action in Teacher Education, 37*(1), 82–98. http://dx.doi.org/10.1080/01626620.2014.970675

Muijs, D., Kyriakides, L., van der Werf, G., Creemers, B., Timperley, H., & Earl, L. (2014). State of the art—Teacher effectiveness and professional learning. *School Effectiveness and School Improvement, 25*(2), 231–256. http://dx.doi.org/10.1080/09243453.2014.885451

Noonan, J. (2016). *Teachers learning: Engagement, identity, and agency in powerful professional development.* Doctoral dissertation, Harvard Graduate School of Education.

Philpott, C., & Oates, C. (2016). Teacher agency and professional learning communities: What can learning rounds in Scotland teach us? *Professional Development in Education, 43*(3), 318–333. doi:10.108/19415257.2016.1180316

Riveros, A., Newton, P., & Burgess, D. (2012). A situated account of teacher agency and learning: Critical reflections on professional learning communities. *Canadian Journal of Education, 35*(1), 202–216. Retrieved from https://cje-rce.ca/

Tschannen-Moran, M. (2014). *Trust matters: Leadership for successful schools* (2nd ed.). San Francisco, CA: Jossey-Bass.

Zepeda, S. J. (2012). *Professional development: What works* (2nd ed.). New York, NY: Routledge.

Zepeda, S. J. (2015). *Job-embedded professional development: Support, collaboration, and learning in schools*. New York, NY: Routledge.

Zepeda, S. J., Parylo, O., & Klar, H. W. (2017). Educational leadership for teaching and learning. In D. Waite & I. Bogotch (Eds.). *International handbook of educational leadership.* (pp. 227–252). West Sussex, UK: Blackwell.

Index

Page references for figures and tables are italicized.

Achieve (organization), 58. *See also* Next Generation Science Standards
action research, 8, *9*
Adam, E., 52, 69, 103
Adamson, F., 17
adult learning, 3, 4, 5, 17, 37, 77, 95;
 agency, 92;
 feedback, 85–86;
 job-embedded learning, 5–6, 60;
 modeling, 84–85;
 principles of, 5–6;
 18, 27, 37;
 reflection, 85;
 relevance, 83;
 self-directed, 83
agency (teacher), 56, 67–68;
 characteristics, 92–95;
 collaboration, 68, 92;defined, 67
Aghasaleh, R., 92
Allexsaht-Snider, M., 92
Allington, R., 77
Amiot, C. E., 37
Andree, A., 16, 38, 76
appreciative inquiry, 11, 93, 94;
 4-D process, 79–80;

means to identify professional development, 2;
research methods, 76
Association for the Advancement of Science, 58. *See also* Next Generation Science Standards
autonomy, 37
Avalos, B., 46

Bakia, M., 68
Bandura, A., 92
Barber, J., 59
Bass, C., 86
Bayar, A., 37
Beijaard, D., 100
Bickmore, D. L., 56
Bocala, C., 70
book study, *9*, 21, 26
Booth, M., 77
Borko, H., 7
Bouwma-Gearhart, J., 58
Breidenstein, A., 6
Brookfield, S. D., 37
Burgess, D., 95
Butler, D. L., 8
Buxton, C. A., 92
Bybee, R. W., 58

Calvert, L., 4, 67, 92
Capps, D. K., 59
Carrejo, D. J., 59
Cervetti, G. N., 59
change of belief structures, 11, 36, 49, *50*;
  instructional practices, 7, 11, 25, 38, 43, 45, 49, 51, 59, 67
Charmaz, K., 62
Chiu, J. L., 61
Choi, Y., 92
Chong, W. H., 76
Choo, C. W., 19
Clarke, H., 79
Coburn, C. E., 18, 19, 27, 28, 59, 66, 68
Cochran-Smith, M., 7
Coggshall, J. G., 6, 12, 17, 18, 27, 30, 37, 60, 77
Cohen, A., 92
coherence, 2, *6*, 11;
  defined, 43;
  job-embedded learning, 5, 16, 60;
  linkages to teacher evaluation and professional learning, 29, 35–36, 38, 43–44, 48–49, 93–94;
  standards, 56
Colestock, A., 18, 27
Collaboration, *6*, 25–26, 30, 59, 92, 94–95, 97–98;
  group goals, 45–46;
  job-embedded learning, 7, 11, 18, 25–26, 28, 37, 38–41
collaborative goal groups. *See* goal groups
Colton, A., 17, 30
Common Core State Standards, 2, 11, 56, 57–59, 61, 63, 66, 69, 93
conjecture mapping, 68–69
constant comparative analysis, 20, 61–62
Constas, M. A., 59
cooperative learning, 38
Cooperrider, D. L., 79, 82
Corbin, J. M., 20, 61

Corcoran, T., 78
Crawford, B. A., 59
Creswell, J. W., 20, 61
Croft, A., 6, 8, 37, 60

Dana, N. F., 7
Darling-Hammond, L., 3, 6, *6*, 16, 17, 18, 27, 36–37, 38, 49, 50, 76, 77–78, 86
Daro, P. F., 78
data analysis: constant comparative method, 20, 61, 62;
  cross-case analysis, 20, 23–26;
  within-case analysis, 20
data collection methods: document review, 5, 40;
  focus groups, 5, 40;
  learning logs, 20;
  participant interviews, 5, 6, 19, 40, 80, 94;
  participant observations, 5, 40;
  shadowing, 19
Datnow, A., 27
Davis, G. A., 18
Day, J. P., 77
decision-making and agency, 92–95
Desimone, L. M., 3, 5, *6*, 7, 38, 59, 77, 78
Dolan, M., 6, 37, 60
Drago-Severson, E., 103
Droph, R., 59
DuFour, R., 52
Duncan, T., 5
Durand, F. T., 61

Eaker, R., 52
Earl, L., 103
edSurge, 7
Egan, B., 79
Elementary and Secondary Education Act of 1994, 57
Ermeling, B. A., 38
Every Student Succeeds Act of 2015, 5;
  job-embedded learning, 5

Fahey, K., 6
Fang, Z., 58
Feiman-Nemser, S., 7
field notes, 61
Firestone, W. A., 60
Fishman, B. J., 8, 56
Fletcher, L., 79
formal learning, 2, 11, 16, 17, 20, 23, 26;
　professional development, 82, 95
Forman, M., 70
Fullan, M., 46, 52, 69, 103

Gabriel, R., 77
Gallagher, L. P., 8, 56
Gallimore, R., 38, 48
Gardner, M., 3, *6*, 77
Garet, M. S., *6*
Gersten, R., 87
Ginsberg, M. B., 17
Glaser, B. G., 20
Glickman, C. D., 6, 17, 36
goal groups, 2, 11;
　cycle of influence, *47*;
　defined, 36;
　goal setting, 37;
　process, *39*;
　self-concordance and goal alignment, 37
goal setting 35, 51;
　adult learning, 37;
　job-embedded learning, 37–38;
　linkages to supervision and teacher evaluation, 93
Goals 2000. *See* Elementary and Secondary Education Act of 1994
Goldenberg, C., 38
Goldschmidt, P. G., 59
Goldstein, D., 57
Gordon, S. P., 17, 36, 59
Gulamhussein, A., 17, 30
Guskey, T. R., 16, 17, 30, 36

Hakuta, K., 58
Hallinger, P., 98

Hamilton, L., 39
Hargreaves, A., 88
Harris, D. N., 36
Hauserman, C., 97
Hensley, F., 6
Higginson, S. K., 8
Hill, H. C., 59
Hirsh, S., 7, 37
Holmstrom, A., 78, 84
Holton, E. F., 77
Hord, S. M., 37–38
Hunzicker, J., 5, 16
Hurd, J., 68
Hyler, M. E., 3, *6*, 77

implications for school leaders, 28–29, 50–51, 67–69, 86–87, 98–102
incoherence and professional learning, 63, 67;
　leader focus, 67–68, 69, 96
informal learning, 2, 17;
　professional learning, 17, 20, 25, 37, 77, 82, 95
intrinsic motivation, 24, 27, 41, 94
Irby, B. J., 59

Jackson, A., 18
Jacques, C., 17, 30
Jagger, S. L., 59
Jimmieson, N. L., 37
job-embedded learning, 18–28;
　adults, 27, 60, 95;
　benefits, 7–8, 18;
　characteristics, 60, 96–97;
　defined, 6–7, 60;
　federal legislation, 5;
　forms, 8, *9–10*;
　middle school teachers, 2, 10–11, 15, 16;
　reflection, 6, 8, 18, 20, 25, 27, 29, 38, 48, 50, 60, 81, 85, 96;
　time, 7, 18, 59, 81–82, 86, 97, 101–2
Johnson, C. C., 38, 66
Johnson, D. W., 38
Johnson, R. T., 66, 67

Jones, B., 68
Jurrow, A. S., 86

Kaufman, J., 66
Kayumova, S., 92
Kendall, J., 57
Keys, T. D., 87
Killian, J. E., 7
Killion, J., 7, 60, 68
Klar, H. W., 98
Knowles, M. S., 77, 83
Koch, J., 59
Kong, C. A., 76
Korbak, C., 56

Lara-Alecio, R., 59
Latham, G. P., 37
Lawson, H. A., 61
Learning Forward, 4, 5
Leary, H., 68
Lee, O., 5, 59
Leo, S. F., 77
lesson study, *9*, 68, 69
Lewis, C., 68
Locke, E. A., 37
Lopez-Prado, B., 56
Lytle, S., 7

MacDonald, E. B., 97
Maeng, J. L., 61
Mangin, M. M., 60
Many, T. W., 52
Martinez, M. C., 60
mathematics and professional development, 12, 76, 78, 81, 84, 94
Mawhinney, L., 28
McGriff, M., 100
McLaughlin, M. W., 6, 18, 27, 37, 77, 86
McQuarrie, F. O., Jr., 17
Means, B., 68
Milton, J., 17, 30
Mitchell, T. D., 27, 28
Mizell, H., 28
Mosher, F. A., 78

motivation and sensemaking, 24, 27, 29
Muijs, D., 98
Murphy, R., 68

National Academies of Sciences, Engineering, and Medicine, 70
National Commission on Teaching & America's Future, 4
National Council of Teachers of Mathematics, 78, 82
National Institute for Excellence in Teaching, 17
National Science Teachers Association, 58. *See also* Next Generation Science Standards
Newman-Gonchar, R., 87–88
Newton, P., 95
Next Gen. *See* Next Generation Science Standards
Next Generation Science Standards (Next Gen), 56, 57–59, 62, 93
No Child Left Behind Act of 2001, 57
Noonan, J., 92

Oates, C., 92
Opfer, V., 66
Orphanos, S., 16, 38, 76

Parise, L. M., 7, 46
Parker, S. L., 37
Parylo, O., 98
Pate, P. E., 18
Pearson, P. D., 59
peer observations, 7, *10*
Penuel, W. R., 8, 56, 68
Perry, R., 68
personalized learning, 95–97
Philpott, C., 92
Polovsky, T., 60
Portfolio, *10*
Powers, E., 7, 37
professional development. *See* professional learning
professional learning, 3, 4–5; costs, 3–4;

deficit approach, 4, 6, 16;
defined, 5, 59–60;
effective professional learning, 2, 5, 6, 12, 15–17, 29; 77;
key features, 16–17, 77–78;
key research, 5, 6, 38;
mathematics, 76, 80, 83;
middle school professional learning, 18;
quick fixes, 3–4
Pruitt, S. L., 58

Quinn, H., 59
Quinn, J., 52, 69, 103

Rasmussen, C., 17, 30
Reflection, 25, 27, 29, 49–50, *50*, 81, 83, 85, 96
reform and professional development, 3, 5, 56, 66–67, 68, 93;
coherence, 38, 60;
policy messages, 66;
standards-based, 57, 69
Reinhartz, J., 59
Reiser, B. J., 56
research methods and approaches, 19–20, 39–40, 61–62, 79–80
Richardson, N., 16, 38, 76
risks and risk-taking, 2, 25, 28, 42, 48, 94, 97
Riveros, A., 95
Ross-Gordon, J. M., 17, 36
Roy, P., 103
Ryan, C., 79

Sandoval, W., 68
Santos, M., 58
Sass, T. R., 36
Saunders, W. M., 38
Scarloss, B., 5
Schnellert, L. M., 8
Schiller, K. S., 61
Schmidt, M., 27
Schwandt, T. A., 40
Schwartz, H. L., 77

science-literacy, 2, 11, 56, 57, 58, 63, 66–67;
research, 59
self-concordance, 37
sensemaking, 2, 11, 15, 16;
job-embedded learning, 19, 20–23, 28;
language-intensive practices, 58;
motivation, 27;
research and theory, 18–20;
teaching identity, 27, 29;
teacher knowledge construction, 1–20;
worldviews, 26–27
Severance, S., 68
Shapley, K. L., 5
Sherin, M. G., 18, 27
Slavin, R. E., 38
Smith, K., 38
Sparks, D., 38
Spencer, D., 58
Spillane, J. P., 7, 46, 59
Stavros, J. M., 79
Stick, S. L., 97
Stonaker, L., 7, 8
Stosich, E. L., 70
Strauss, A. L., 20, 61
study groups, 7, 10
studying student work, *10*
Sumner, T., 68
Surrette, T. N., 68
Swanson, R. A., 77
synergy 2, 35;
between individual and collaborative work, 35, 42, *43*;
propelling learning, 47–48

Taylor, M. J., 87–88
teacher agency, 56, 92;
affirmation of teacher as decision-maker, 93–94;
champions personalized learning, 95;
characteristics, 92–93;
collaboration, 94–95;
defined, 67–68;

professional learning, 91–92;
support structures, 95
teacher evaluation xiii, 2, 36;
coherence, 48–49;
coupled with professional
learning, 39;
goal setting, 37, 39, 43, 50–51;
purpose, 51
teacher identity, 27, 29;
core features, 100
teacher networks, 40, 42, 46, 48
teacher quality, 16–17, 36–37
Thompson, K. F., 18
Thompson, L., 66
Tienken, C. H., 7, 8
Tong, F., 59
Toyama, Y., 68
transfer of skills, 17–18, 26, 27, 60, 83, 85–86, 97
trust, 60, 97
Tschannen-Moran, M., 97, 103

U.S. Congress, 57

Valdés, G., 59
Verloop, N., 100
Vermunt, J. D., 100
von Frank, V., 7, 103

Voogt, J., 68

Waring, S. M., 60
Wei, R. C., 16, 38, 76
Weick, K. E., 18, 19
Wertz, F. J., 80
Wheeler, L. B., 61
Whitfield, B. L., 37
Whitney, D., 79
Whittier, C., 39
Whitworth, B. A., 61
whole-faculty study, *10*
Wilcox, K. C., 61
Wlodkowski, R. J., 17
Wood, D. R., 37
Wood, F. H., 7, 17
Woulfin, S. L., 18, 28

Yamaguchi, R., 8
Yendol-Hoppey, D., 7
Yin, R. K., 19
Yoon, K. S., 5, 8, 16
Yore, L. D., 59

Zepeda, S. J., 3, 4, 7, *10*, 16–17, 18, 27, 28, 37, 39, 48–49, 59, 60, 77, 83, 86, 92, 96, 97, 98

About the Editor

Sally J. Zepeda, PhD, is a professor at the University of Georgia in the Department of Lifelong Education, Administration, and Policy. She teaches courses related to instructional supervision and theory, teacher evaluation, and professional development. She is a former high school English and speech teacher, middle and high school assistant principal, principal, and director of special programs. She has published 30 books and many articles and book chapters.

Her books include *Instructional Supervision: Applying Tools and Concepts*, which was simultaneously translated into Turkish; *Job-Embedded Professional Development: Support, Collaboration, and Learning in Schools*; and *Supervision: New Perspectives for Theory and Practice*, coedited with Jeffrey Glanz.

She has worked with many school systems in the United States and overseas, especially in the Middle East, to support teacher and leader development. She has received numerous local and national awards including the University Council of Educational Administration Master Professor Award.

About the Contributors

Michael P. Cassidy, PhD, is a senior researcher for the STEM Education Evaluation Center (SEEC) at the Technical Education Research Centers in Boston, Massachusetts. His research interests are teachers' professional learning, the impact of STEM educational programs, and the application of computational thinking across content areas. Dr. Cassidy has worked on multiple National Science Foundation and Institute for Education Science grants. His work has been funded by the Office of Naval Research and the Rhode Island Foundation.

Jen Cole, EdD, is a K–6 literacy specialist in the Madison County School District in Danielsville, Georgia. Before this she was a building-level instructional coach and classroom teacher. She received the Ponsoldt Chair for Elementary Teaching Award and the Excellence in Teaching Award from the Clarke County Foundation for Excellence as well as the Ray E. Bruce Academic Support Award from the Department of Lifelong Education, Administration, and Policy at the University of Georgia.

James M. Meneguzzo, EdD, has been an educator for almost 20 years. He has served in many roles, including middle and high school mathematics teacher, assistant principal, and principal. He received his doctorate in educational leadership from the University of Georgia where he was awarded the Mullins Award in recognition of his leadership achievements. He has spoken at regional and national conferences on engaging instructional strategies, STEM, and instructional coaching.

Brandi Wade Worsham, PhD, is an assistant professor in the College of Education at Brenau University in Gainesville, Georgia. Her research interests include middle school education, the professional development of preK–12 educators, and the acquisition of content knowledge and pedagogy of pre-service teachers. Her scholarship has appeared in *The Encyclopedia of Middle Grades Education* and *Handbook of Research on Teacher Education and Professional Development*.

www.ingramcontent.com/pod-product-compliance
Lightning Source LLC
Chambersburg PA
CBHW030144240426
43672CB00005B/265